'What is art?'

...it could be anything at all.

CALVIN TOMKINS

Art Without Artists is published in conjunction with an exhibition of the same title curated by John Foster and Roger Manley for the Gregg Museum of Art & Design, September 27–December 16, 2012. A presentation of ARTS NC STATE.

ISBN 978-0-9831217-1-8

DESIGN: TOKY Branding + Design, St. Louis, Missouri, USA
EDITOR: Chis Vitiello
PRINTED BY: Four Colour Print Group

Printed in USA

FRONT COVER: *Handmade Letter for Sign,* 20th century, Belgium, wood, electrical sockets, wire, 12" x 8 1/2" x 1 1/2", collection of John and Teenuh Foster

INSIDE FRONT COVER: *Found Object,* 20th century, United States, ball of string, shoelaces, electrical wire, 5" x 3", collection of John and Teenuh Foster

INSIDE BACK COVER: *Ghost Man in Forest,* c. 1945, United States, silver gelatin snapshot (accidental double exposure), 5" x 3", collection of John and Teenuh Foster

BACK COVER: *Make-do Backpack,* c. 1945, United States, wood chair back, wool shirt, axe, sleeping bag, rope, 36" x 17" x 8", collection of John and Teenuh Foster

ART *without* ARTISTS

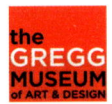

JOHN FOSTER, ROGER MANLEY

Gregg Museum of Art & Design, Raleigh, North Carolina

Foreword

Every art museum must be selective about what it collects, since it's obviously impossible to preserve or display examples of everything. The collecting process inevitably focuses on acquiring objects that are the rarest or most representative, the most beautiful, the most well-made and the most valuable, as far as it is within the means of the institution or its donors to do so. With luck and perseverance, the results can be impressive but also, to many visitors, often a bit daunting. After a few hours spent surrounded by masterpieces and confronted with major achievements, they may go home thinking of art only as something made by geniuses or highly trained masters and only to be admired in a pristine setting under special circumstances.

The Gregg Museum of Art & Design, sited at a land grant university like NC State, offers a good place to question this assumption, since it's no great leap from the land grant idea—that almost anyone can become more useful and better citizens if they are afforded an opportunity to get a higher education—to the concept behind *Art Without Artists:* that almost anything can be enjoyed as art, and indeed become art, if given an opportunity to be appreciated as such.

The emphasis on geniuses and masters is already downplayed at museums like the Gregg where, besides the paintings and sculptures, the vast majority of things in its collection—textiles, garments, ceramics, photography, furniture, metal, wood, glass, design objects, self-taught art, and tribal and ethnographic artifacts—are by anonymous or unknown makers. Moreover, most of them were originally slated for uses far removed from being displayed in a gallery. The Gregg's clothing and textiles were by and large meant to be worn, or draped over surfaces; the ceramics were once intended to hold liquids or accompany meals; the furniture was meant to be sat-on or worked-at; most of the tribal objects were made to insure survival by aiding with food production or invoking the gods.

Now installed in a new context (a museum), they've already been re-purposed as objects intended to educate, inspire, entertain, and delight anyone who pauses to look at them. This is scarcely different from asking the same thing of the rocks, snapshots, farm implements, industrial artifacts and other objects that guest curator John Foster has gathered for *Art Without Artists*. Ideally, after viewing them the alert and perceptive visitor may discover that the world outside the gallery seems to offer more frequent opportunities to experience art, too.

We at the Gregg are grateful to Chris Vitiello, who edited much of the text in this book, and to all the lenders to the accompanying exhibition—Aarne Anton of American Primitive Gallery, William Brack, Shari Cavin and Randall Morris of Cavin-Morris Gallery, Steve Erenberg of the Radio-Guy Museum, Jim Goodnight of SAS Institute, Randy and Linda Marcuson, the North Carolina Transportation Museum, NC Department of Transportation, NC State University's College of Engineering Constructed Facilities Laboratory, the Marine, Earth and Atmospheric Sciences Department, and the College of Agriculture and Life Science's Insect Museum—but most of all to John Foster, who proposed, co-curated, and energized *Art Without Artists* out of his lifelong curiosity about the world around him. He has not only brought strange and exciting bits of that world into the museum, but, along with his team at TOKY Branding + Design (who collaborated on this publication), has brought the exhibition out into the world as well.

Child's Toothbrush, c. 1955, United States, plastic, 3 1/2" x 6" x 3/4", collection of John and Teenuh Foster

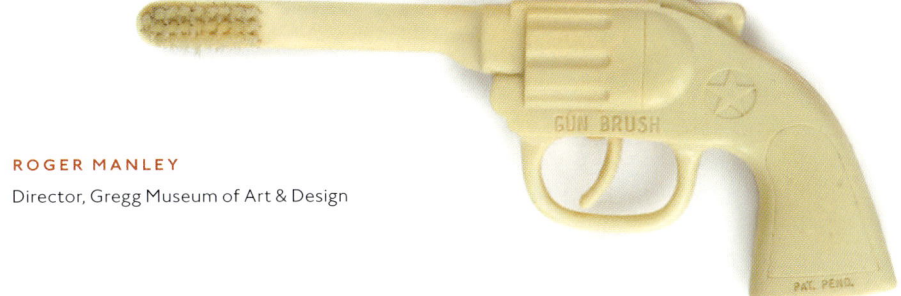

ROGER MANLEY
Director, Gregg Museum of Art & Design

The Power in Things

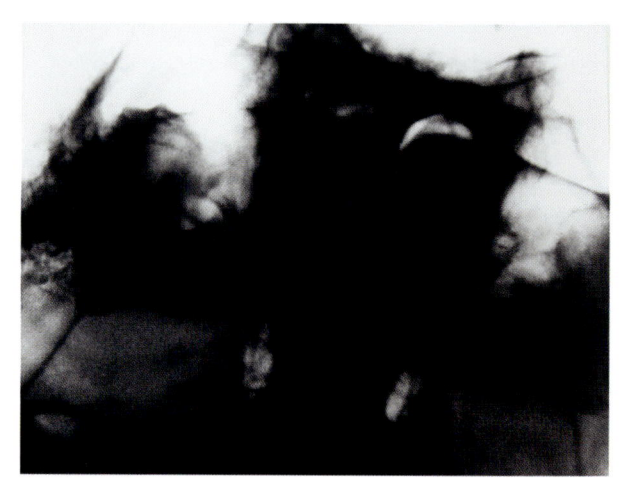

6 *Landscape,* 1974
photograph from
found X-Ray,
John Foster, United
States, silver gelatin
print, 16" x 20",
private collection

Almost 40 years ago, in 1974, I was throwing trash in a dumpster behind my studio in south St. Louis when I noticed a large brown envelope. It had been laid conspicuously on top of other refuse, almost as if someone wanted it to be found. I pulled out the contents and was delighted to be looking at what turned out to be medical X-rays: large 16 x 20 inch acetate—like sheets of black and clear images of bones, chests and body parts. As a photographer, painter and Master of Fine Arts degree candidate at Washington University, I was instantly intrigued by the possibilities these anonymous images presented.

In the hands of an artist, and not a medical professional, these X-ray images had now flipped places—from science to art. What once had been a source of medical insight into arthritis, broken bones or other human maladies, was for me something new and altogether different. Back in the photography studio, these X-ray photographs of bones and tissue became my negatives. I produced large abstract prints of body parts that I interpreted as landscapes. Exhibited at my MFA thesis show in 1976, these landscapes echoed their surreal and ethereal connection to the human body, displaced and reinterpreted once again.

I remember several years later I was taking photographs near a construction site when I made another startling discovery—what seemed to be a large, freeform sculpture was resting discarded on a raw concrete floor. Though "in reality" it was only a hardened glob of pink expanding insulation foam—perhaps left by some worker who had only cleaned out his injection hoses directly onto the ground at the end of his shift—in my reality it was already a work of art, and only needed a change of context in order to be appreciated. Sure that no one would miss it (and in fact, the worker was probably glad to discover it gone) I picked it up and took it home to hang on my studio wall, where it immediately became another treasure in my growing collection.

Found objects have always held a fascination for me. As a young boy, I collected things that I could find for free. I found rocks of varying shape and color in creeks, and poached all kinds of flowers from neighbor's yards, my favorite being the iris. Bird eggs fascinated me, speckled, tans, and especially the robin's egg, which presented a blue so perfect I know of no other blue like it even today.

Though at the time I wasn't able to fully articulate what was happening, I can see now that I was looking intently at the world around me and creating taxonomies in order to compare one object against another. These were the seeds of connoisseurship—where I could begin to discern differences, similarities, and make judgments regarding rarity and value.

It was the beginning of my lifetime search for objects that hold enigmatic qualities. I bore easily, so if something can't keep my attention for a year or so, I eventually replace it. Being a serious collector is a commitment and a journey—always seeking, learning, refining and comparing. The frustrating—but also exciting—part is that I know my collection can (and will) never have a finish line. I may discover what I think is the best snapshot I have ever seen, but I know there will always be a better one, or at least a different one that's just as intriguing, right around the corner.

With that in mind I continue to seek objects with unexplained origins, extraordinary forms, rich patinas, and startling designs. More than anything else, I look for things that seem to possess an aura of mystery, for their unanswered questions and tantalizing clues allow me to experience wonder. Objects that cross boundaries and collide with culture, objects that are not easily defined, objects with surrealist overtones—these become my power objects. With these around me, at least I am never bored.

JOHN FOSTER
Guest Curator, St. Louis, MO | September 2012

Painting is dead!

MARCEL DUCHAMP

Art Without Artists

ROGER MANLEY

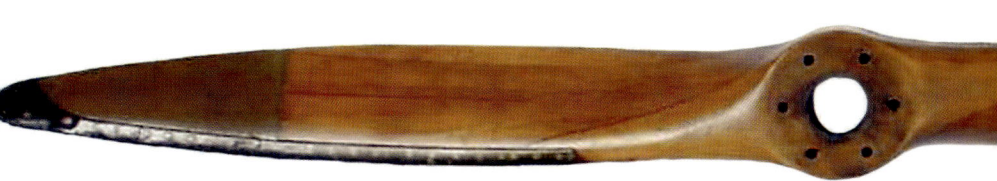

The essence of the principle of the 'uncarved rock' is that things in their own original simplicity contain their own natural power, power that is easily spoiled and lost when that simplicity is changed.

BENJAMIN HOFF, *The Tao of Pooh*

Airplane Propeller, 1940, United States, laminated oak, brass, fabric, 83" x 7", courtesy of North Carolina Transportation Museum, Spencer, NC

A hundred years have passed since Marcel Duchamp visited a 1912 Paris exhibition about the then-new field of aviation technology and came home seeing the world through even more opened eyes. Astounded by what he had seen, he described one object in particular to fellow artists Fernand Léger and Constantin Brâncuşi: "Painting is dead! Who can make "anything better than that propeller? Tell me, can you?" The precise curve of the propeller's wooden blades, determined by the aerodynamic requirements of flight,[1] had struck Duchamp as both aesthetically pleasing and intellectually stimulating. Seeing it displayed on its own, detached from the prow of a plane, he could appreciate it as a new kind of sculpture.[2]

A few months later, Duchamp mounted an inverted bicycle wheel on a stool so that he could enjoy the pleasing arrangement of its radiating spokes and suspended rim, and watch the moving shadows it threw on the walls of his studio as he spun it. The creation was almost casual. "I liked to look at it," he said, "just like I liked to look at flames dancing in the hearth."[3] "It was just a distraction. I didn't have any special reason to do it, or any intention of showing it, or describing anything. No, nothing like that..."[4] Although the original version of this piece was never exhibited (and eventually lost), in time he would regard it as the first in a series of some thirty objects he later called his *Readymades.* He coined this term to suggest that these objects were works of art that he had found "as-is" rather than fabricated himself.[5]

Other examples soon followed. In 1914 he purchased a bottle drying rack (*porte-bouteilles*) in the basement hardware division of the great Paris department store BHV.[6] Hauling it back to his studio, he placed it on a pedestal and then asked his friend Man Ray to photograph it as if it were sculpture. It had concentric tiers of metal bands with uplifted prongs intended for draining and drying empty bottles neck downward. Taken out of its usual context (the kitchen sink of a *brasserie*) and studied on its own, the bottle rack—which he renamed *Hérisson* ("Hedgehog") or *L'Égouttoir* ("The Drainer")—could conjure up other associations. Depending on what thoughts or memories were already in the mind of the observer, it might look like a miniature metal evergreen tree, some kind of strange torture instrument, an abstracted crown, an architectural model, some kind of steel tiara, or an exercise in pure form. By treating it as sculpture, it began to look like a sculpture.

Another hardware store purchase (this time, in New York) was a standard American snow shovel with a metal scoop and wooden handle, on which Duchamp wrote *En prévision d'un bras cassé* ("In Advance of the Broken Arm") and then suspended on a string from the ceiling, where its large curved blade would slowly revolve with the air currents. Some visitors seeing it dangling above them were reminded of a cresting wave or a square-rigged vessel under sail (the heraldic symbol of Paris), while others compared it to the guillotine or the Sword of Damocles, threatening to fall and cut them at any moment.

Duchamp realized that the unexpected placement was key to the viewers' new appreciation of the shovel's shape and potential meanings. When taken down and leaned against a wall, it immediately turned back into an ordinary snow shovel. But dangling overhead, its poetic inscription hinted at an *impending* history, as if it were evidence of some mishap about to take place instead of one that had already happened.

Over the next few years Duchamp found other evocative industrial objects and gave them provocative titles and new contexts to yield still more *Readymades.* These included a steel comb (*Peigne*), a rubberized Underwood typewriter cover (*Pliant de Voyage* or "Traveler's Folding Item"), a coat rack (which he called *Trébuchet* or "Trap") and a revolving metal chimney vent (which he surreally entitled *Pulled at Four Pins,* a literal translation of "tire a quatre epingles," a French phrase roughly equivalent to "dressed to the nines"). Ambiguities provoked by their redisplay in odd new contexts—like nailing the coat rack to the floor or dangling a hat rack from the ceiling—made them as visually arresting as they had once been potentially useful.

In 1917 Duchamp purchased a white porcelain urinal from a bathroom fixtures company. After rotating it 90 degrees to mount it horizontally, he titled it *Fountain* and entered it as a work of art in that year's Society of Independent Artists exhibition at New York's Grand Central Palace, under the pseudonym of "Richard Mutt." His fellow Society members were far from amused, and viewed the repurposed urinal as a deliberate and impudent insult to what they had intended as a serious art event. Despite the annual show's claim to be open to all, the exhibition committee partitioned "R. Mutt's" sculpture from public view on the grounds that it was immoral, vulgar and plagiarized.[7]

Duchamp withdrew it immediately and then published an objection (under his own name) claiming that a urinal was no more immoral than a bathtub. "It's the kind of thing you can see any day in the display window of a plumbing supply store," he pointed out. As for being plagiarized, Duchamp wrote, whether or not Mr. Mutt had "...made the fountain with his own hands or not has no importance. He CHOSE it. He took an article of life, placed it so that its useful significance disappeared under the new title and point of view [and] created a new thought for that object."[8]

He took an article of life, placed it so that it's useful significance disappeared ...[and] created a new thought for that object.

"Of course," as Umberto Eco points out, "underlying such selections there is an intention to provoke, but also the persuasion that every object (even the lowest variety) has formal aspects that we rarely pay any attention to. As soon as they are singled out, 'focused,' and offered to our attention, these objects take on an aesthetic significance, as if they had been manipulated by the hand of an author."[9] By suggesting that the artist could be freed from the task of physically creating an art object, and by showing how things like context, date, originality, authorship, authenticity, handwork, value or expertise may raise as many questions as answers, Duchamp touched off a host of controversies in the art

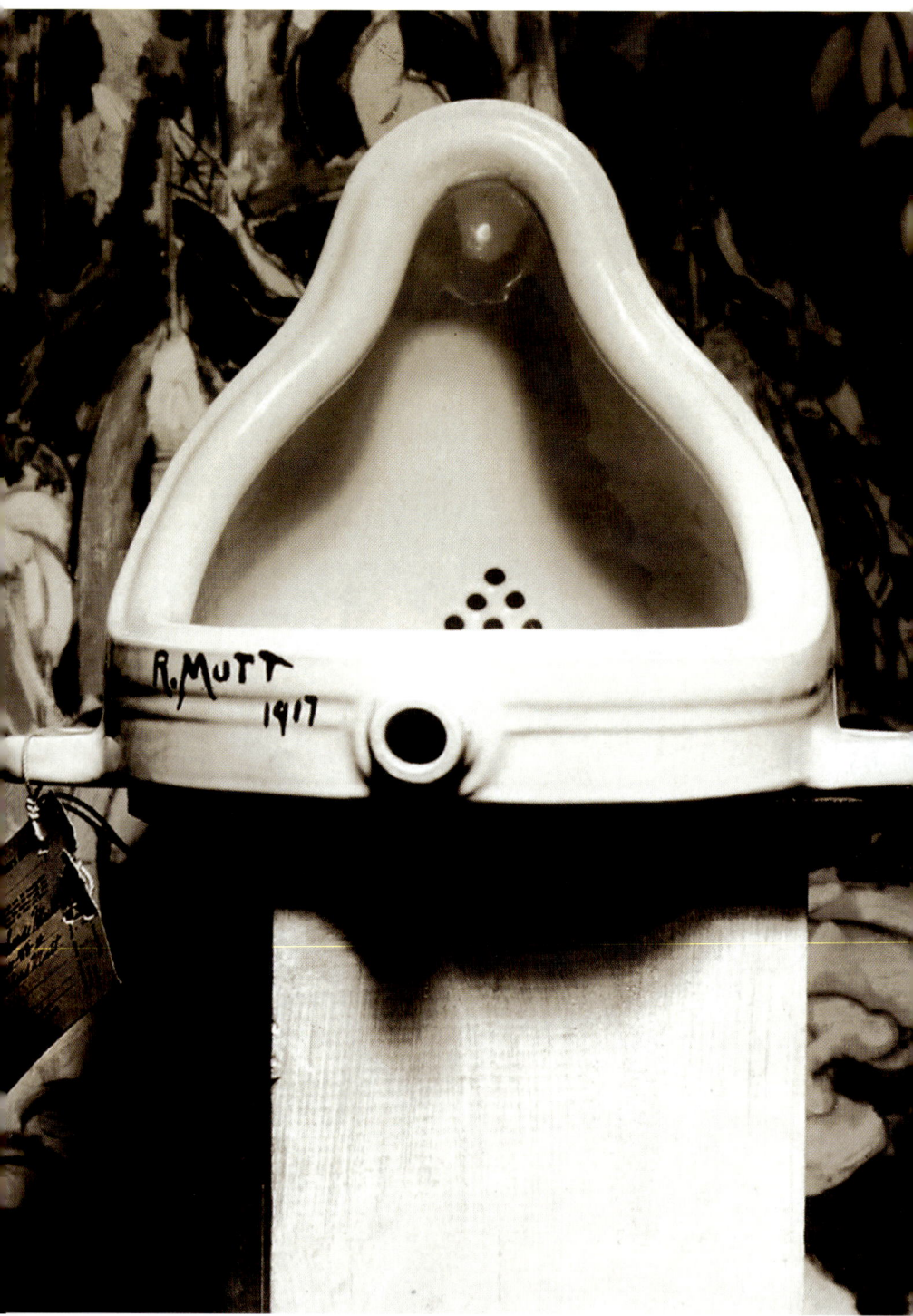

world that continue to this day, even though appropriation and context-shifting is a far more common strategy in art-making now than in his time.

Art critic Calvin Tomkins says that Duchamp's *Readymades* "...posed the question 'What is art?' and suggested, quite disturbingly, that it could be anything at all..."[10] According to historian Kristina Seekamp, "By questioning the traditional definition of art and the artist, Duchamp made people reconsider them and bring them to the realization that art is an institution wholly defined by social constructs. There is nothing that comes to this world naturally termed as 'art.' Art is a matter of opinion and perspective, and is defined by its past as well as continuing traditions."[11]

While Duchamp certainly shook the New York art world with his upstart exhibition entry, he was hardly the first to realize that art is largely subjective. In 1757 David Hume wrote (in *The Standard of Taste*) that, "Beauty is no quality in things themselves: It exists merely in the mind which contemplates them; and each mind perceives a different beauty. One person may even perceive deformity, where another is sensible of beauty; and every individual ought to acquiesce in his own sentiment, without pretending to regulate those of others."[12] In other words, one man's trash may be another man's art.

In any case, Duchamp himself never arrived at a clear definition or explanation for what his *Readymades* were, preferring to say only that they were a way of "denying the possibility of defining art."[13] By opening up the definition of what art could be, he helped open the eyes of artists, critics, collectors, curators and historians to a whole new range of alternatives that would eventually have a major impact on the history of art. This perspective helped pave the way for much that would follow, from Dada, Surrealism, and Conceptual Art to kinetic sculpture, Carl Andre's firebricks and Andy Warhol's soup cans and Brillo boxes.[14]

The *Readymades* were, for the most part, utilitarian industrial products. For although he could see the disconnect between artists and art-object making, Duchamp still saw art as something that had to have been made by *someone,* if not by self-proclaimed artists. "Art, etymologically speaking, means to 'make,'" he wrote. "Everybody is making, not only artists."[15]

—

The impulse to regard certain found objects as aesthetically pleasing and intellectually stimulating (i.e., as art)—even if no artist had any role in creating them—began millennia before Duchamp's

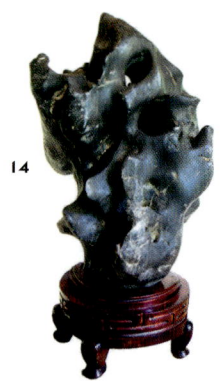

bicycle wheel. It also extends far beyond manmade objects to include things in which no human intervention was involved at all, other than to change their context or put them on display.

Many centuries ago, for example, Chinese Han Dynasty scholars and connoisseurs[16] began erecting weirdly eroded limestone boulders in their gardens and mounting smaller rocks on pedestals for contemplation and appreciation. Called *gōngshí,* the abstract forms of the stones were appreciated for the variety of associations they might conjure up, from things like leaping fish, swimming turtles or birds in flight, to hermit caves and seated deities. Similar traditions later developed in Korea *(suseok)* and Japan *(suiseki)* where stones that could hint at waterfalls, cliffs, islands and mountain ranges were particularly admired. In Zen gardens, raked gravel simulating ocean waves helped complete the effect of miniature landscapes.

Scholar's Stone,
c. 18th–19th
centuries, China,
found water-shaped
limestone, 23" x 15"
x 14", collection of
Randy and Linda
Marcuson

Outright imitation was to be avoided, however, for it was important to the Daoist and Zen literati who collected them that the shaping hands of human intervention not be evident. Because of this, most early examples were naturally occurring rocks with no alterations. Later, as demand rose and suitable stones became harder to find, pieces were often first worked by hand to give nature a head start, and then reburied or lowered back into lakes to let natural weathering finish the job by eroding the tool marks and developing seemingly time-worn natural patinas.[17]

The ideal stone should appear as if found in its natural state so as not to distract from its ability to seem to transform from one state of being to another: i.e., looking like a mere, accidentally-formed rock one instant, and then calling up an entire landscape (or animal, or deity) the next.[18] This subtle shifting back and forth in perception was thought to suggest the simultaneous physical and spiritual nature of reality itself. By gazing meditatively at such stones and letting themselves see them first one way and then the other, the scholars who owned them could achieve an expanded perception that they believed was essential to seeing the world as it is.

The famously ambiguous duck/rabbit image used in early gestalt psychology illustrates a similar perceptual transformation:

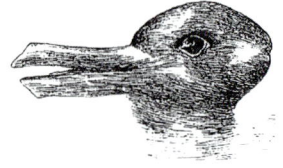

The subject of a gestalt demonstration knows that his perception has shifted because he can make it shift back and forth repeatedly while he holds the same book or piece of paper in his hands. Aware that nothing in his environment has changed, he directs his attention increasingly not to the figure (duck or rabbit) but to the

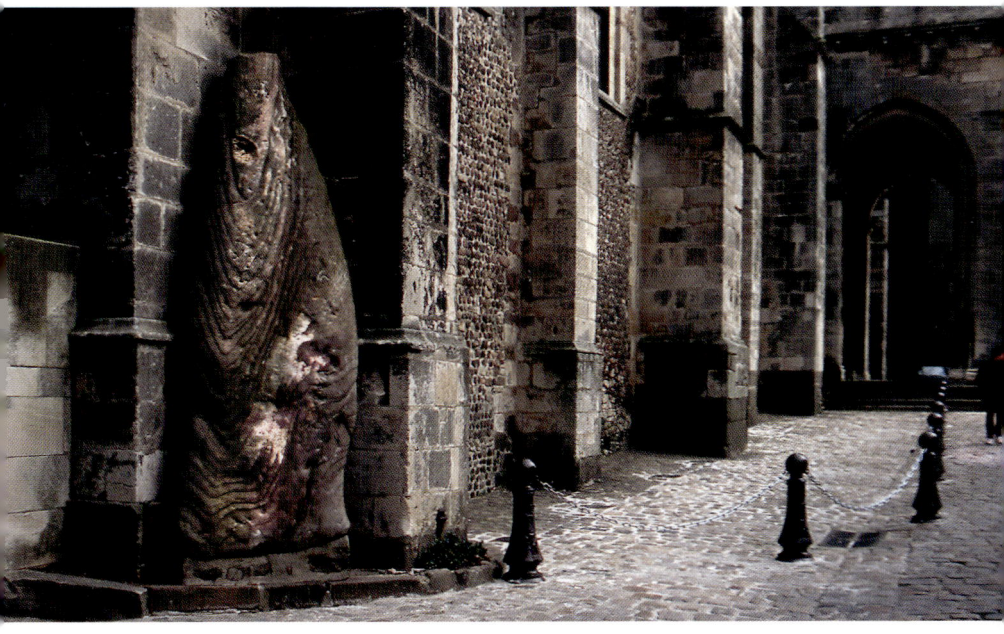

lines of the paper he is looking at. Ultimately he may even learn to see those lines without seeing either of the figures, and he may then say (what he could not legitimately have said earlier) that it is these lines that he really sees but that he sees them alternately *as* a duck and *as* a rabbit.[19]

St. Julian's Stone, c. 3500 BCE, Le Mans, France, photo by Roger Manley, 1999

Asians weren't the only ancients who took advantage of shape-shifting rocks to enhance their beliefs about the physical and spiritual duality of the world. Leaning against the exterior wall of the 9th century gothic cathedral of St. Julian in Le Mans, France, is a 15-foot-tall prehistoric menhir popularly known as "Saint Julian's Stone," weathered in such a way that it resembles a tall figure draped in flowing robes. The pre-Christians who discovered and erected it almost certainly saw it that way, too. Throughout northern Europe are other ancient, naturally-formed standing stones that resemble human (or supernatural) figures, animals, genitalia, feet, vessels, portals, and other unusual shapes whose original associations were forgotten long ago. Similar stones have been found throughout the rest of the world as well.[20] Preserved in place mainly because of their sheer size and weight, stone circles can perhaps be seen as among the few remaining early examples of found object collecting.

Wealthy Renaissance collectors were also appreciative of objects that appeared to fluctuate between the realms of accident (i.e., nature) and intention (or artifice), although they didn't associate found objects with belief and perception in quite the same way as Chinese scholars, or even as their own medieval Christian or pagan forbears. Mineral specimens with clusters of cubic crystals resembling the roofscapes of Mediterranean villages, polished slabs of hard Florentine limestone (*pietra paesina*) that looked like miniature paintings of craggy landscapes, dendritic agates that seemed to contain ferns embedded in translucent crystal, or branches of coral that formed rough crosses the color of Christ's blood were eagerly sought after and traded-for as they assembled their *Kunst-und-Wunderkammern* ("Art and Wonder Chambers"), the cabinets of curiosities that became the precursors of today's museums. While not as concerned as their Far Eastern counterparts with avoiding all evidence of human intervention—a marble panel with swirls of mineral inclusions suggesting clouds might be enhanced with angels painted in by hand—the attribute of looking like a found accident of nature while also looking like an intentional work of art was especially appealing to collectors whose world view demanded evidence of the handiwork of a divine Creator in everything surrounding them, from nature to the world of human industry.

The shift in perception that occurs whenever found objects seem to transform from non-art to art and back again provides the "alternating current" that is the primary source of such objects' visual power—that, and the associations generated whenever they are seen (even momentarily) as something other than what they were to begin with.

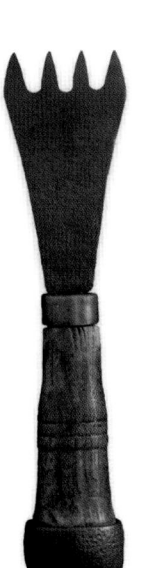

Ice Pick, c. 1930, United States, metal, wood, 8" x 2 ½", collection of John and Teenuh Foster

For example, when mounted on a pedestal an ice pick, with a form determined solely by the physics involved in breaking ice, might pass for a shaman's idol except for the fact that a nearby label explains its original purpose. Its seeming transformation is encouraged, of course, by its display in a new context (like a gallery or museum), where viewers are primed to think that surely there must be more to this object than "just" an ice pick.

Quite a few "modernday readymades" achieve their visual power through associations with art made by artists. A patched textile —its pattern determined only by necessity and the availability of scraps of cloth—can look as intentionally composed as any collage. A toothbrush shaped like a gun can seem as surreal as any intentional Surrealist work. The random calligraphic effects of ink blotting could resemble a sketch by Mark Tobey or Jack Tworkov, while an unpainted paint-by-number image—naked and machine-like in its blue and numbered outline topography—might recall certain works by Andy Warhol or Paul Bridgewater.

Or is it the other way around? Since Duchamp, artists have opened our eyes to new ways of finding art in our surroundings, too. Anyone who has seen Picasso's 1943 bicycle-seat-and-handlebar assemblage, *Bulls' Head,* or his 1951 bronze, *Baboon and Young,* may never look at automobiles or bikes quite the same way again. Works like Jean Dubuffet's intentionally crude, graffiti-like paintings and the compacted automobile wreckage of John Chamberlain's sculptures have even made it possible to appreciate the strange beauty of urban blight.[21]

Perhaps nothing has achieved that to such a degree as photography, which can render everything from the sublime vistas of Ansel Adams's Yosemite to Walker Evans's auto junkyards or Sebastiao Salgado's sweating miners equally capable of being appreciated aesthetically. It is also the most democratic of art forms, since nearly everyone takes pictures and shares images, while few become sculptors or painters. Susan Sontag has pointed out how photography, once thought to be the most mechanical, least handmade medium, results in some of the purest "found art" of all. And more often than not, amateur snapshots are even better at achieving this than self-consciously "fine" images.

> Surrealism lies at the heart of the photographic enterprise: in the very creation of a duplicate world, of a reality in the second degree, narrower but more dramatic than the one perceived by natural vision. The less doctored, the less patently crafted, the more naïve—the more authoritative the photograph [is] likely to be. Surrealism has always courted accidents, welcomed the uninvited, flattered disorderly presences. What could be more surreal than an object which virtually produces itself, and with a minimum of effort? An object whose beauty, fantastic disclosures, emotional weight are likely to be further enhanced by any accidents that might befall it?[22]

Such accidents include everything from the alligatored cracks that form in the emulsions of old glass-plate negatives and the acid yellowing of old silver prints to more catastrophic historical events that leave their mark upon the photographs. Whole exhibitions have consisted of found photos discovered after the 9/11 and Katrina disasters, in which the contrast between the images of graduations, birthday parties and loved ones gathered around the Christmas tree is made more poignant, surreal and seemingly "meaningful" by the obvious damage the prints, like their subjects, have suffered. In far-more-common cases, where the fates or situations of the people seen in snapshot images remain unknown,

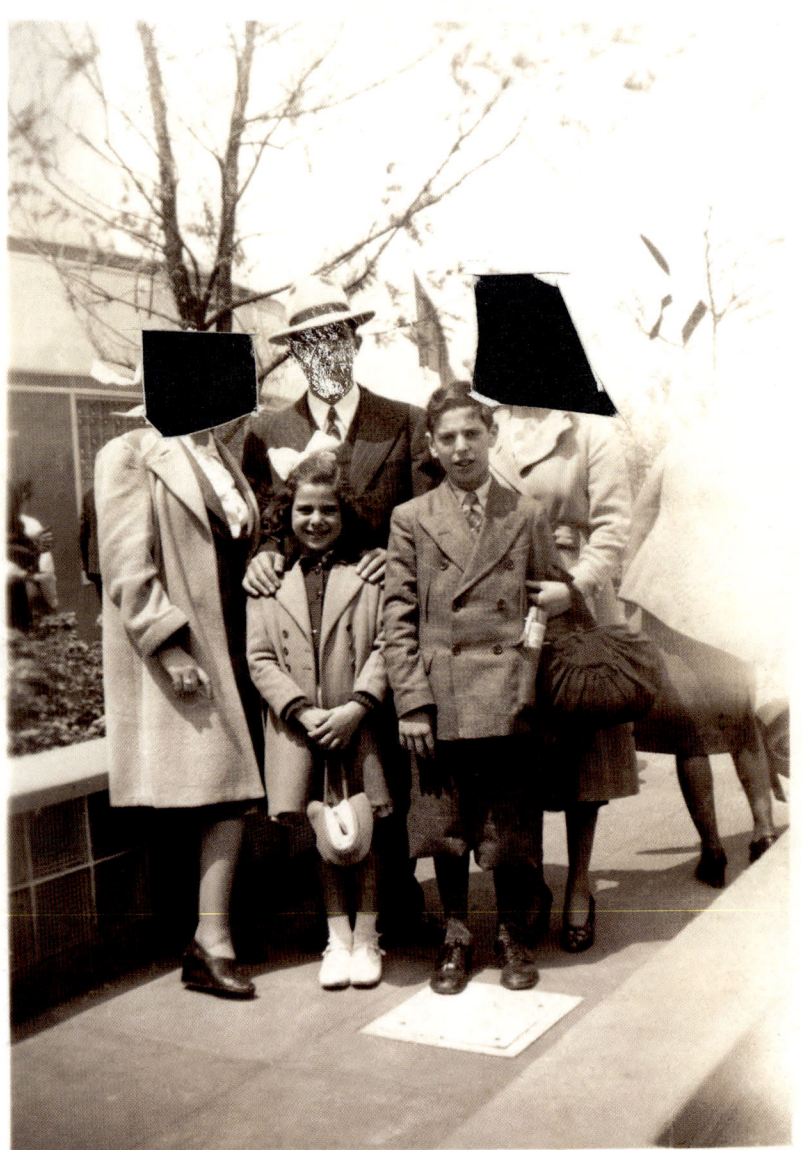

viewers are free to make their own associations (or invent explanations), just as they do with any other found objects.

Recovered or found photos are, in fact, doubly-found works, since the act of taking a picture in the first place is one of taking a piece of reality (the light of the moment) and bringing it home. "To take a photograph," Sontag wrote, "is to participate in another person's (or thing's) mortality, vulnerability, mutability. Precisely by slicing out this moment and freezing it, all photographs testify to time's relentless melt."[23]

LEFT: *Unpopular Relatives*, c. 1955, American, silver gelatin snapshot, 4 1/2" x 3", collection of John and Teenuh Foster

Indeed, providing evidence of that melt—time's inescapable insistence on transforming everything that exists from one state to another—lies at the heart of all found art, and is what allows certain everyday objects to call attention to the most central of life's processes: change, aging and decay unto death. It lies at the heart of most other art as well. Bronze sculptors, for instance, discovered early-on that newly-cast sculpture, glitteringly brassy and metallic, can seem almost anaemically lacking in presence, but that corrosive substances like salt, sulfur, vinegar or animal urines could produce rich patinas that lent an aura of antiquity to their works by invoking the power of natural, time-impacted experience. The same impulse lies behind things as disparate as rusticated masonry, "faux" finishes, and Shabby-Chic styling. Decorators know that even the most severely clinical of chrome-and-white-carpet urban apartments needs a few bowls of ikebana, ammonites, or crude, y-shaped Dogon ladders to introduce enough signs of nature, time and age to make them begin to seem habitable.[24]

time's inescapable insistence on transforming everything that exists... lies at the heart of all found art

Time and transition are what the ancient stone circles measured, what the Renaissance artists struggled to capture, what the Han scholars could glimpse by contemplating their eroded stones and what Duchamp expressed in his painting, *Nu descendant un escalier n°2*, in which a faceless figure seems to be yielding to time and gravity, shuffling downwards toward entropy.[25] He began to see it in his *Readymades* too: the spun bicycle wheel slows to a stop, having gone nowhere. Lying horizontal or nailed to the floor, the urinal and coat rack are left useless, their original purposes no longer served. Just as every tree and creature falls, every stone seeks equilibrium, time and gravity conquer all.

If this were all, the message of found objects and old photos might be relentlessly depressing. But in fact each transformation is really only a moment in a much larger cycle: discarded clothes may first become rags, those rags become a quilt, which *then* (in a new art context) becomes a wall hanging, which may then inspire anyone who sees it to view their own old cast-offs in a new way. The art context feeds back upon the utility context the moment someone inspired by the wall hanging returns home from the gallery to turn their own castoffs into a quilt. At that point the whole cycle becomes a kind of counter-thermodynamic perpetual motion machine.[26]

art's first requirement is an open mind ...we may all gain by becoming artists

Seen in this same light, Duchamp's descending nude offers a more hopeful image too, since its depiction of multiplicity and simultaneity suggests that time and entropy will be overcome. Meanwhile, almost a century after R. Mutt's *Fountain* so puzzled and outraged its unprepared audience, its message continues to reverberate, repeating the real lessons it has left us with: that art's first requirement is an open mind, and that we may all gain by becoming artists—by keeping our eyes open and "finding" the world as well.

1. Or at least as far as those were understood at the time, not even a decade after the Wright brothers' first successes at Kitty Hawk in 1903.

2. Brâncuşi may have been struck by it as well, since a few years later customs officials seized some of his own bronzes as illegally-transported airplane parts when he attempted to ship them to an international exhibition.

3. Marcel Duchamp, in *Marcel Duchamp*, The Museum of Modern Art and Philadelphia Museum of Art, 1973, p. 270.

4. Pierre Cabanne, *Dialogues with Marcel Duchamp*, New York: Viking, 1971, p. 47.

5. In fact, while many were simply found or identified, others required a little work. Art historians like Arturo Schwarz, Juan Antonio Ramirez, André Gervais and Thierry Duve have developed a whole taxonomy for the *Readymades*, categorizing some of them as "pure" (unaltered found objects that were "already made" when he chose them), "impure" (assembled or altered; multiples and reproductions), "ephemeral" (lost, undocumented and/or may never even have existed in the first place; only described or named as if a title alone were enough), "documental" (paper transactions), etc. There is no universally-agreed-upon scheme, however, and recognized *Readymades* range from more than fifty to fewer than twenty examples.

6. Bazar de l'Hôtel de Ville, directly across the street from the Paris City Hall.

7. Historians like William Camfield have mentioned that there may also have been some fear that visitors might actually mistake it for a functioning urinal and be tempted to use it. Such a fear might not have been unfounded, either. Several artists—among them Kendell Geers, Björn Kjelltoft, Pierre Pinoncelli—did succeed later in "using" replicas of the work installed in retrospective exhibitions, before claiming their acts of voiding as homage or as performance art. If homage, they may have missed the point since Duchamp was presenting a new use for the fixture, not the one for which it had been originally designed.

8. Juan Antonio Ramirez, *Duchamp: Love and Death*, Even, London: Reaktion Books, 1998, p. 54.

9. Umberto Eco, *History of Beauty*, Alastair McEwen trans., New York: Rizzoli, 2010, p. 406.

10. Calvin Tomkins. *Duchamp: A Biography.* New York: Henry Holt, 1996, p. 159.

11. Kristina Seekamp, "Unmaking the Museum: Marcel Duchamp's *Readymades* in Context," in *toutfait.com, Marcel Duchamp Studies Online Journal*, volume 1, 2005.

12. David Hume, *Essays, Moral, Political, and Literary* (1741–83), Eugene F. Miller ed., 2nd edition, Indianapolis: Liberty Classics, 1987, p. 230.

13. Tomkins, p. 159, and Seekamp, p. 1.

14. In 2004, a survey of more than five hundred art historians elected Duchamp's *Fountain* as the most influential work of 20th century art. See Charlotte Higgins, "Work of art that inspired a movement... a urinal," *The Guardian*, December 2, 2004.

15. Dalia Judovitz, *Unpacking Duchamp: Art in Transit*, Los Angeles: University of California Press, 1995, p. 110.

16. The Han Dynasty extended from 206 BCE to 220 CE.

17. Duchamp often reworked and altered his *Readymades*, too, understanding that the effect is always more important than how it was achieved.

18. Stones that could be repositioned in various ways—stood on end to suggest one set of associations, displayed horizontally for another—were especially treasured, and scholars sometimes commissioned several pedestals for a single prized rock to accommodate different ways of displaying it.

19. Thomas Kuhn, *The Structure of Scientific Revolutions*, Chicago: University of Chicago Press, 1962, p. 114.

20. Found objects of wood, shell and other materials were equally appealing and also used as objects of contemplation, but other than some venerated pieces of contorted driftwood and gnarled roots carefully preserved in Asian temple collections, most of them rotted away long ago. This undoubtedly left objects made of stone disproportionately represented.

21. Examples could be extended almost infinitely. Seekamp also singles out Charles Scheeler, William Carlos Williams, and Edgar Varese, but there are thousands of others.

22. Susan Sontag, *On Photography*, New York: Delta, 1977, p. 56.

23. Sontag, p. 15.

24. Chris Vitiello has also pointed out that "someone compelled to surround himself with new objects responds to their fear of death by denying time's inexorable forward elapsation, as if rewinding back to the beginning of a timespan with each purchase of a glistening object fresh from the process of its pro-duction." [Personal correspondence, July 25, 2012]

25. *Nude Descending a Staircase No. 2*, painted in 1912 and exhibited at the New York Armory in 1913. Now in the collection of the Philadelphia Museum of Art.

26. Vitiello, op. cit., 7/25/12.

OVERLEAF: *Le Masque-Douche*, c. 1930–40, France, steel, plastic, 60" x 30" x 4", collection of Steve Erenberg; intended for facial cleaning.

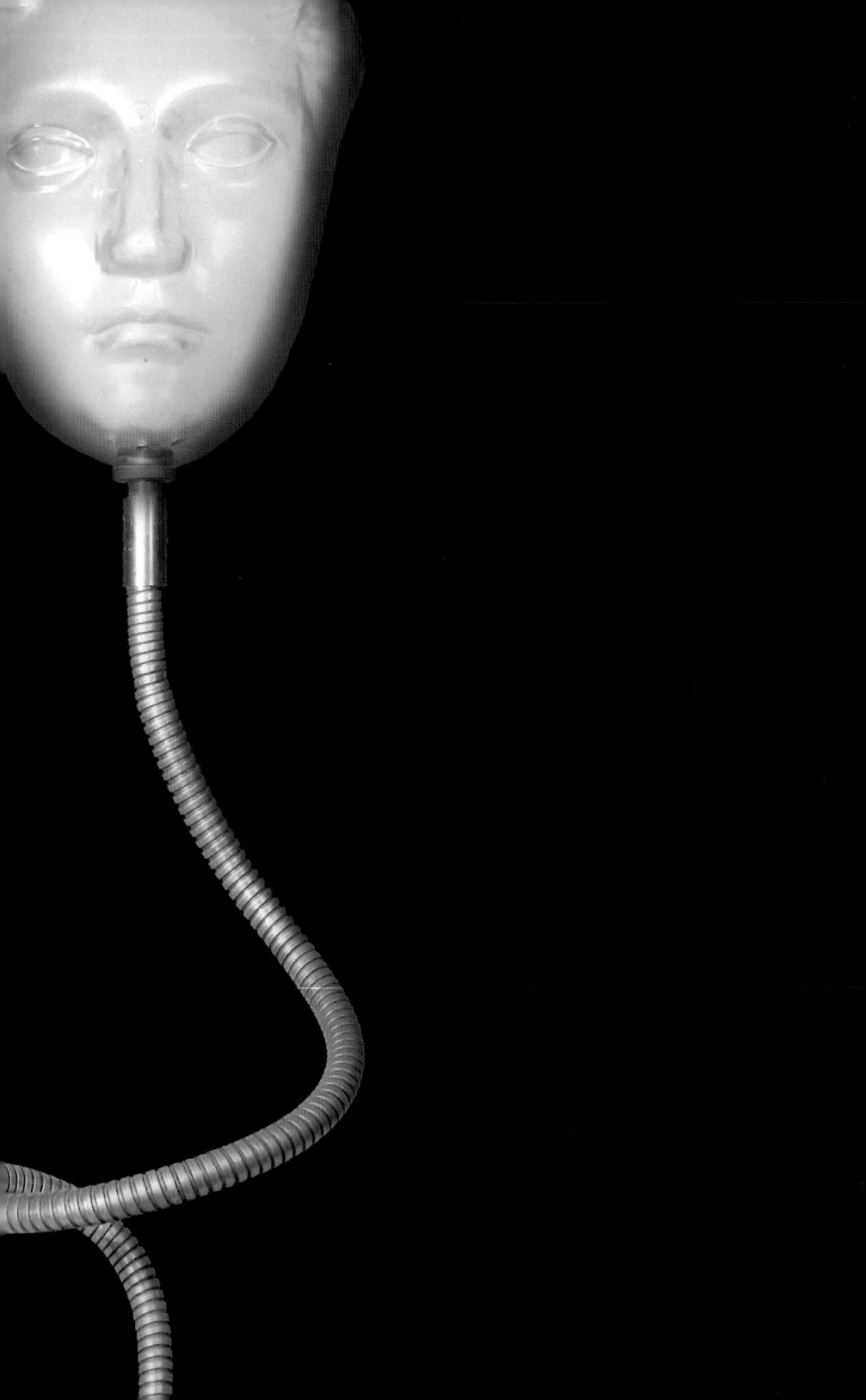

OBJECTS

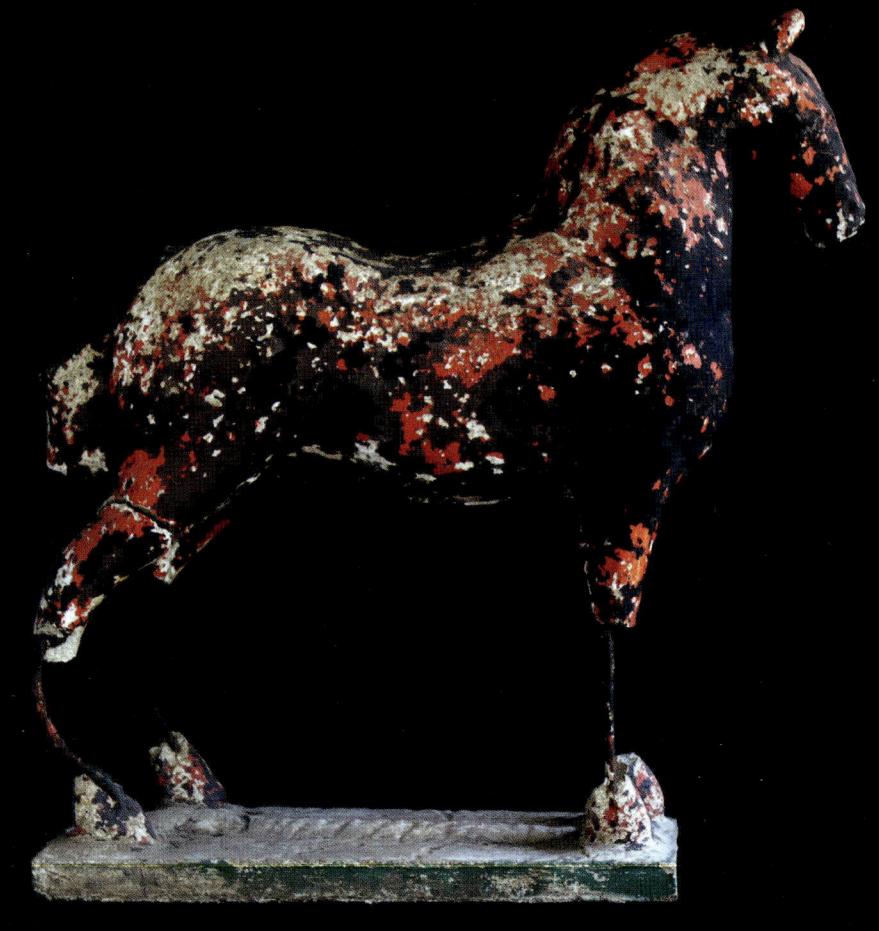

YARD SCULPTURE, c. 1950, United States, cast and painted concrete,
25" x 28" x 8", collection of John and Teenuh Foster

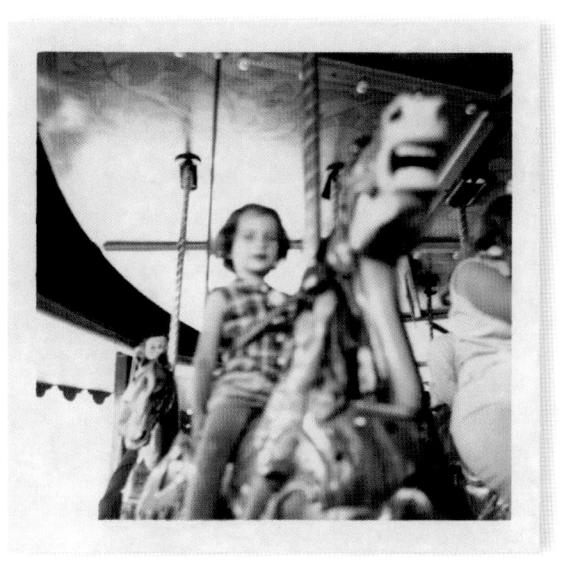

CAROUSEL HELL RIDE, c. 1955, American, silver gelatin snapshot,
3 ½" x 3 ½", collection of John and Teenuh Foster

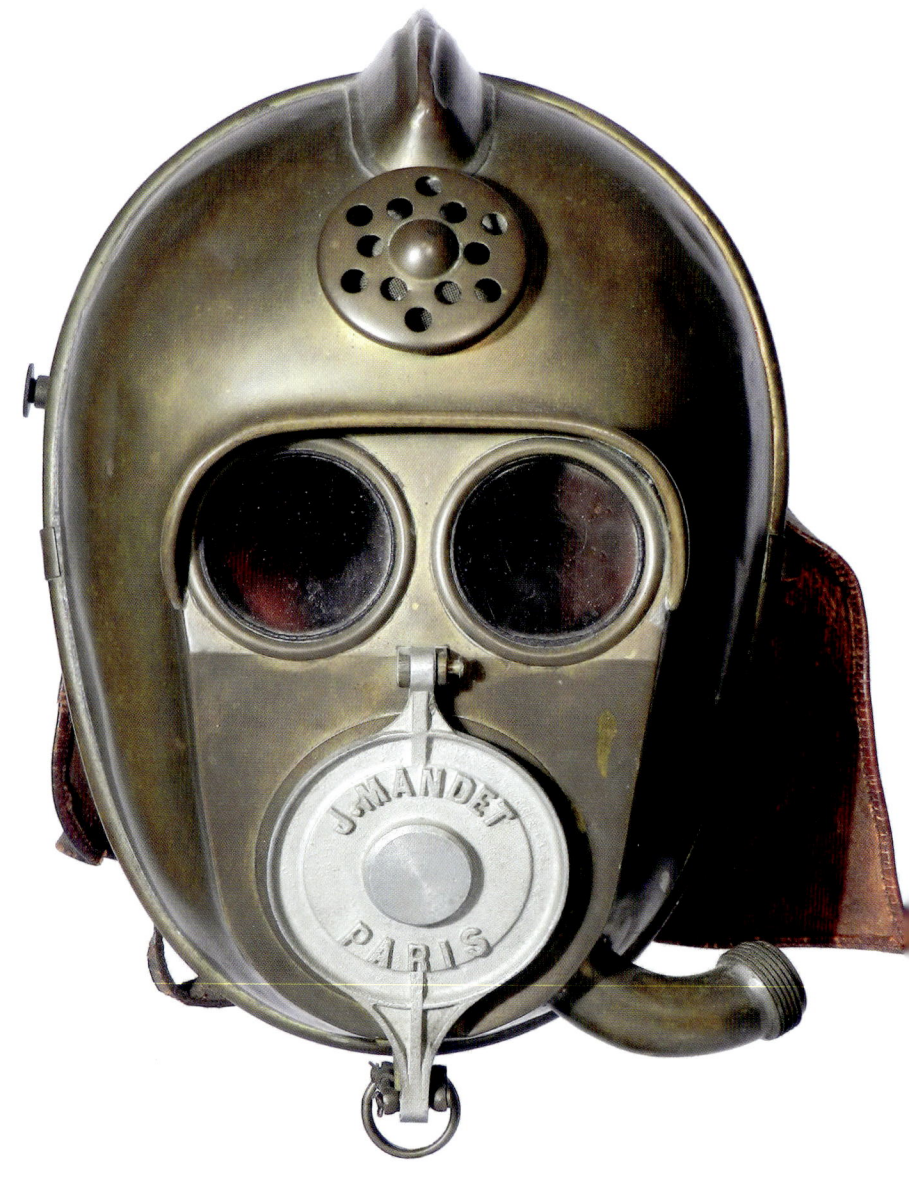

FIREFIGHTER'S RESPIRATOR MASK, 1918, France,
brass, leather, mica, rubber, 12" x 9" x 10", collection of Steve Erenberg

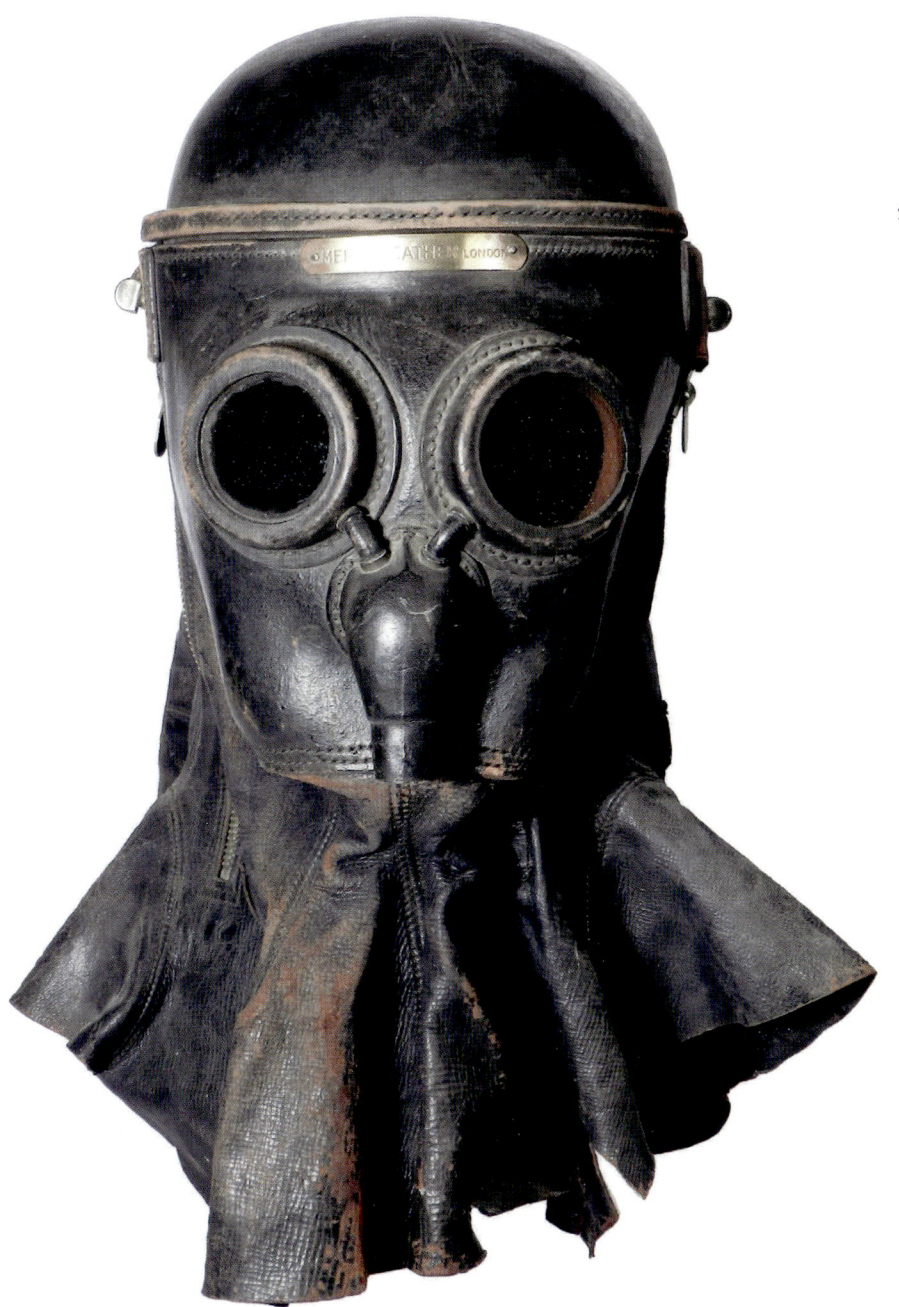

FIREFIGHTER'S RESPIRATOR MASK, 19th century, England, brass, leather, mica, 16" x 8" x 11", collection of Steve Erenberg

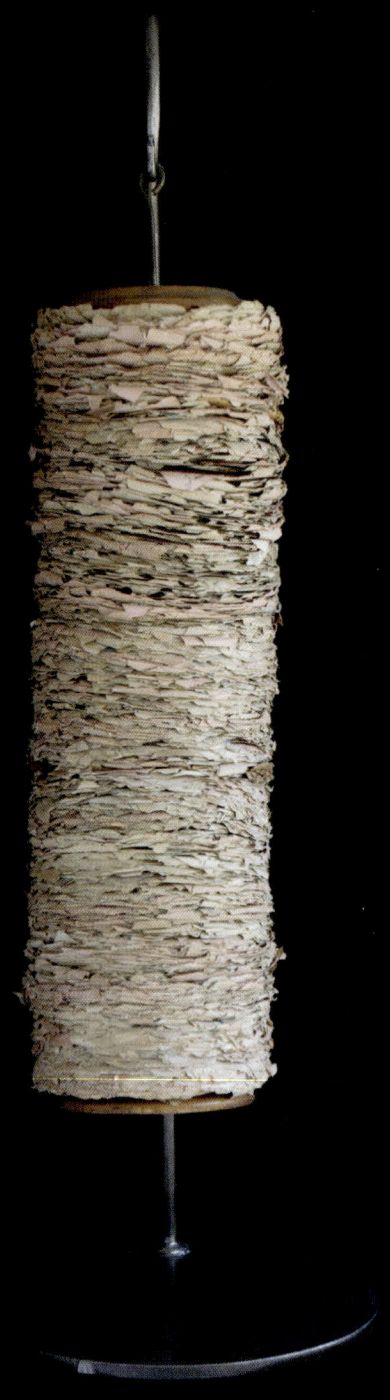

SPOOL OF DRUGSTORE PRESCRIPTIONS, 1951, United States,
paper bills on wire, wood, 24" x 7" diameter, collection of John and Teenuh Foster

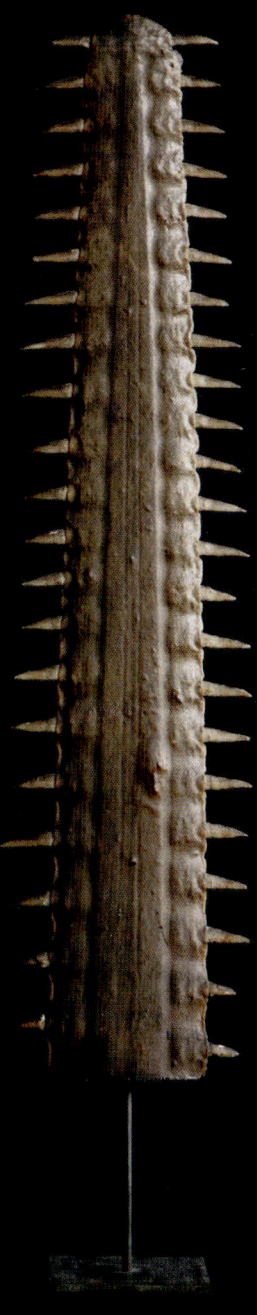

SAWFISH BILL (Carpenter Shark rostrum), vintage oceanic object,
bone, 26" x 6 ½" x 1", collection of John and Teenuh Foster

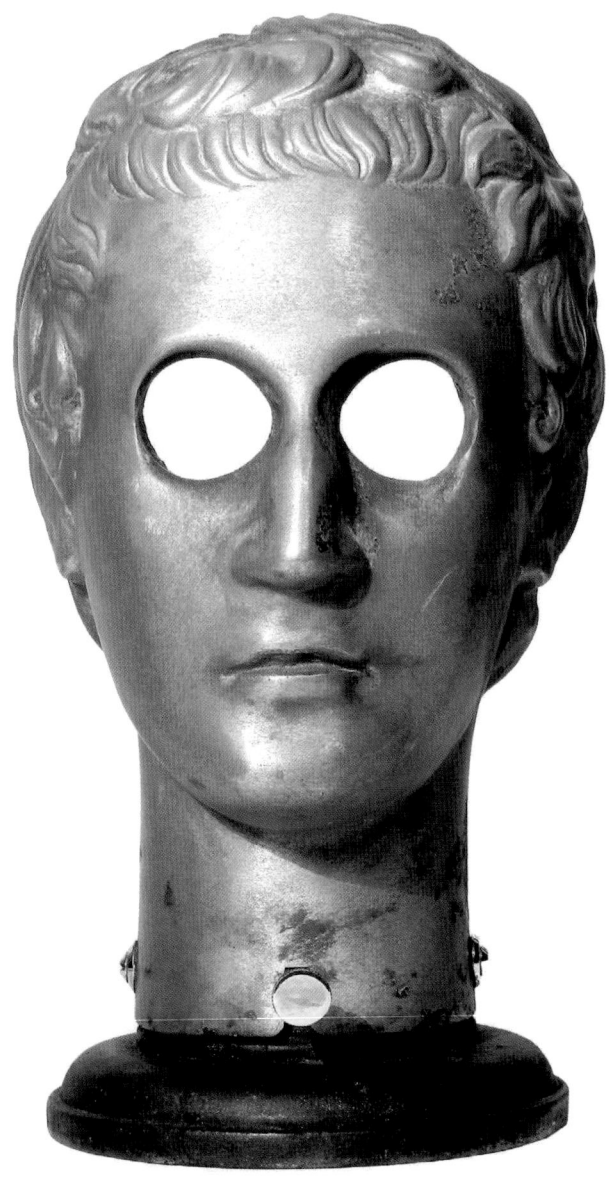

OPHTHALMOPHANTOME, c. 1880, United States,
aluminum, cast iron, brass, 12 ½" x 6" x 6", collection of Steve Erenberg;
used with cadaver or pig eyes to practice ophthalmic surgery.

Across: **MAN WITHOUT EYES**, c. 1940, United States,
silver gelatin photo booth prints, 2" x 1 ½" each, collection of John and Teenuh Foster

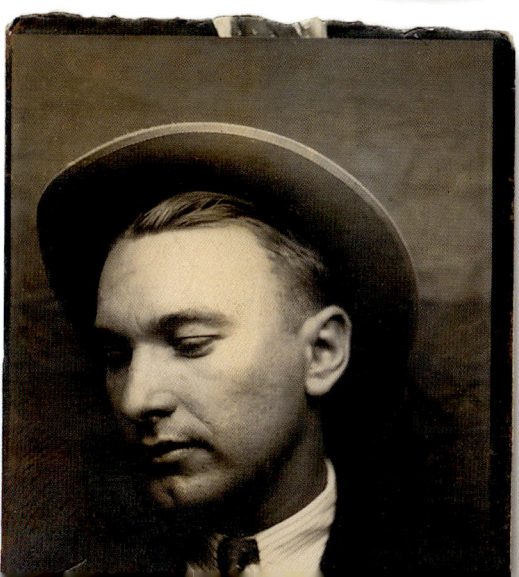

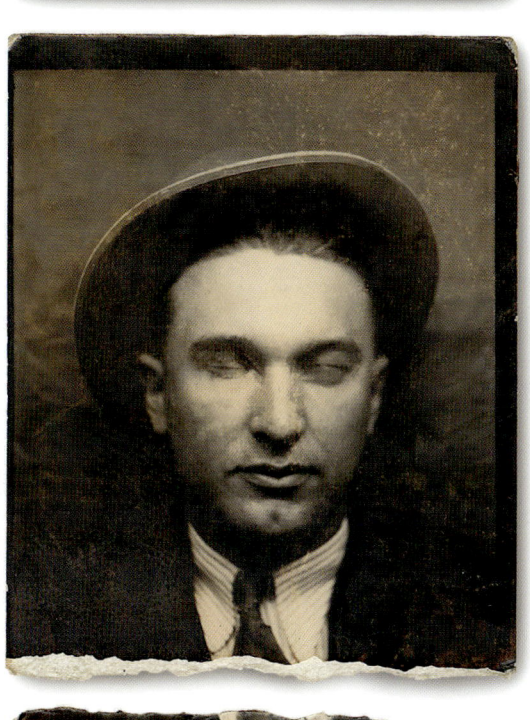

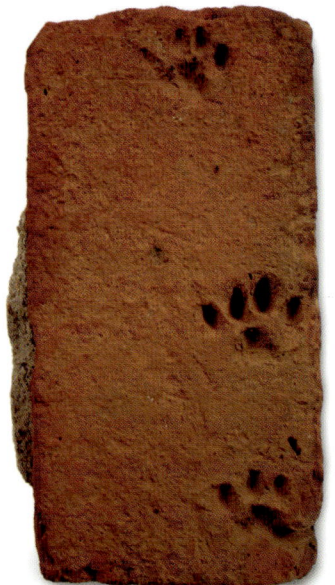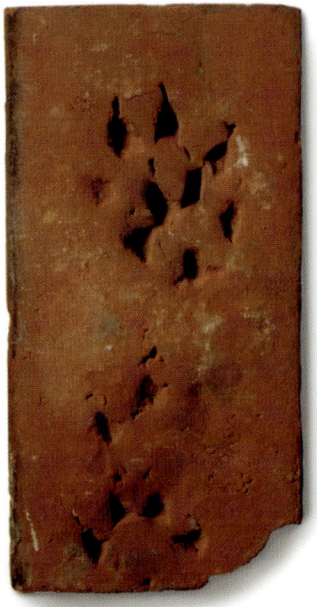

HANDMADE BRICKS, 19th century, United States,
sun-dried clay, 8" x 4" x 2 ¼", collection of John and Teenuh Foster

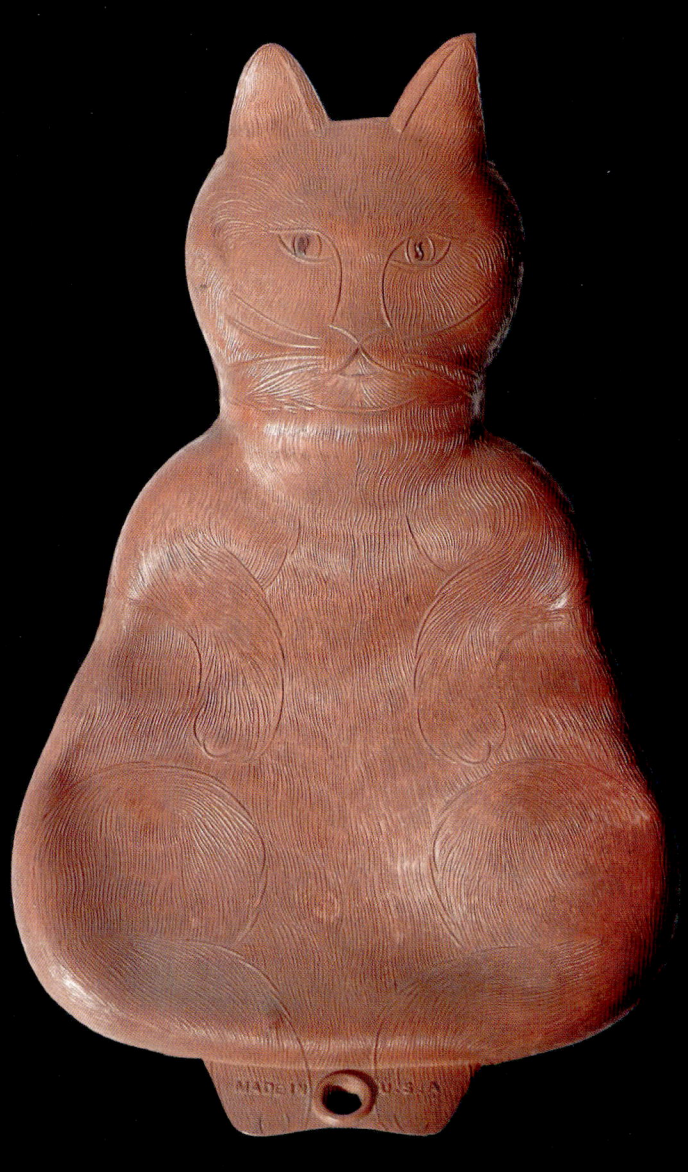

HOT WATER BOTTLE, c. 1930, United States, rubber,
12" x 8", collection of Steve Erenberg

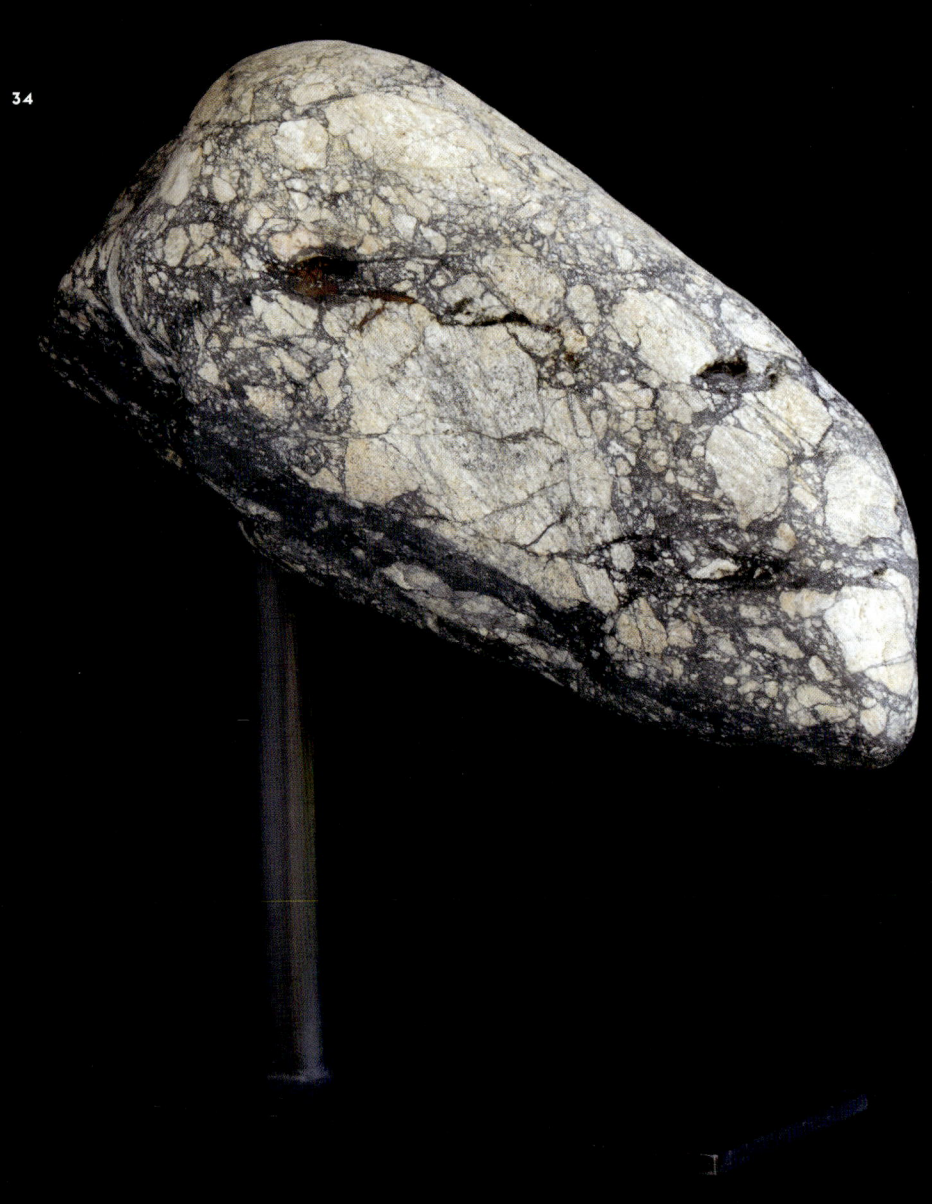

FOUND ROCK HEAD, United States, natural stone,
6" x 12" x 5", collection of John and Teenuh Foster

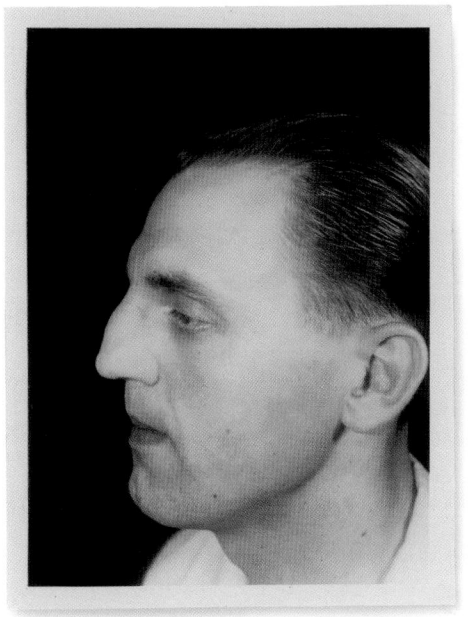

PROFILE, c. 1940, United States, silver gelatin snapshot,
3 ½" x 2 ½", collection of John and Teenuh Foster

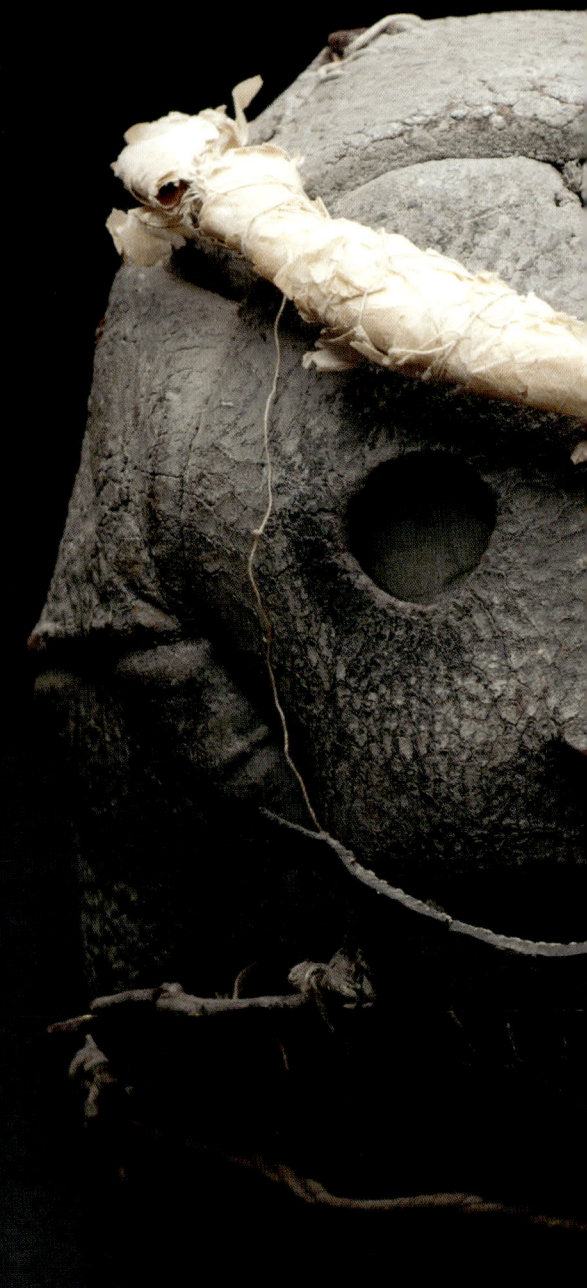

CEREMONIAL MASK, 20th century, Mexico, soccer ball,
paper, twine, 7 ½" x 8 ¼" x 8", collection of Shari Cavin and Randall Morris

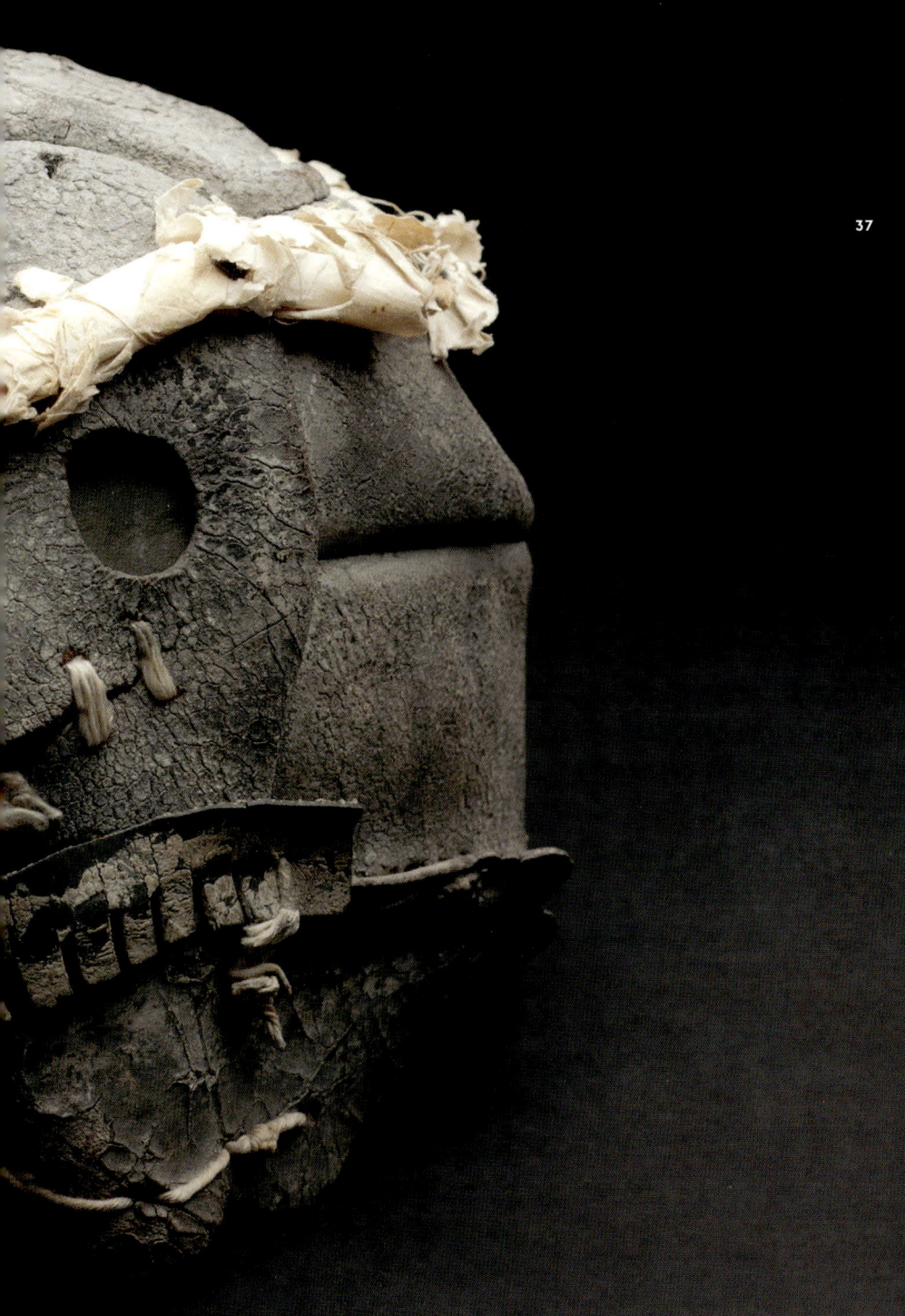

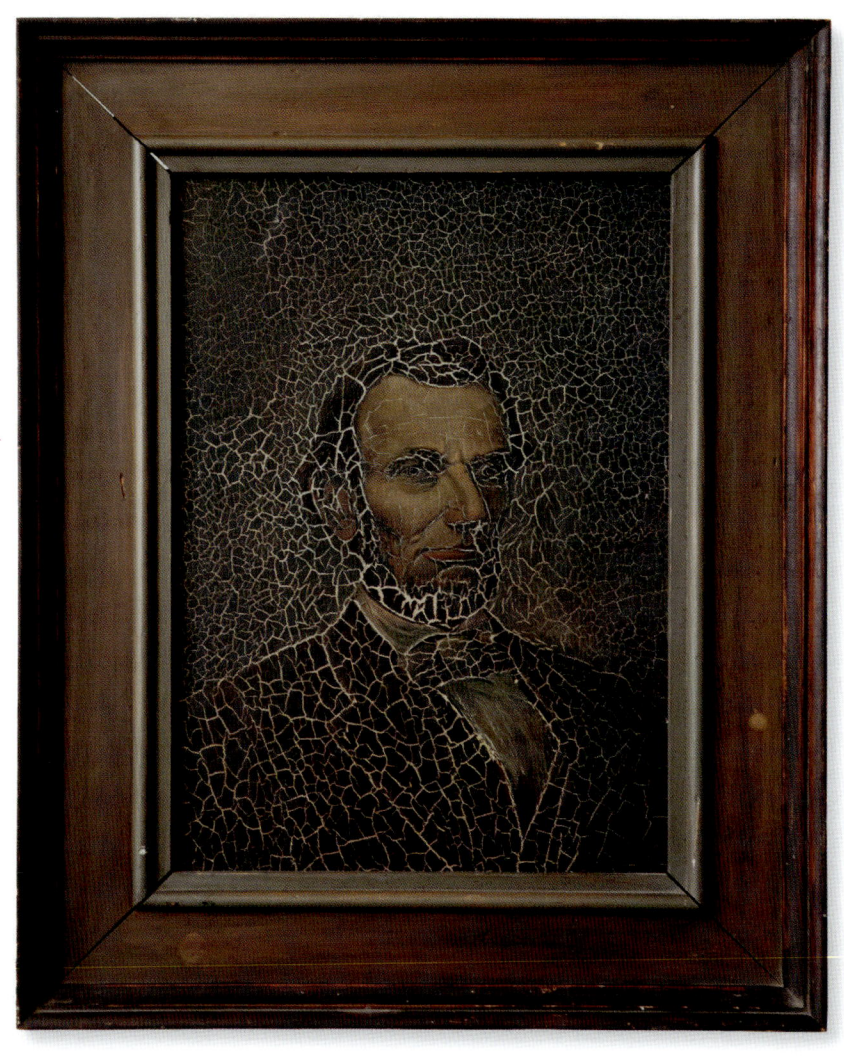

ANONYMOUS PAINTING OF ABRAHAM LINCOLN, C. 1930s,
United States, oil on canvas, 26" x 18", collection of John and Teenuh Foster

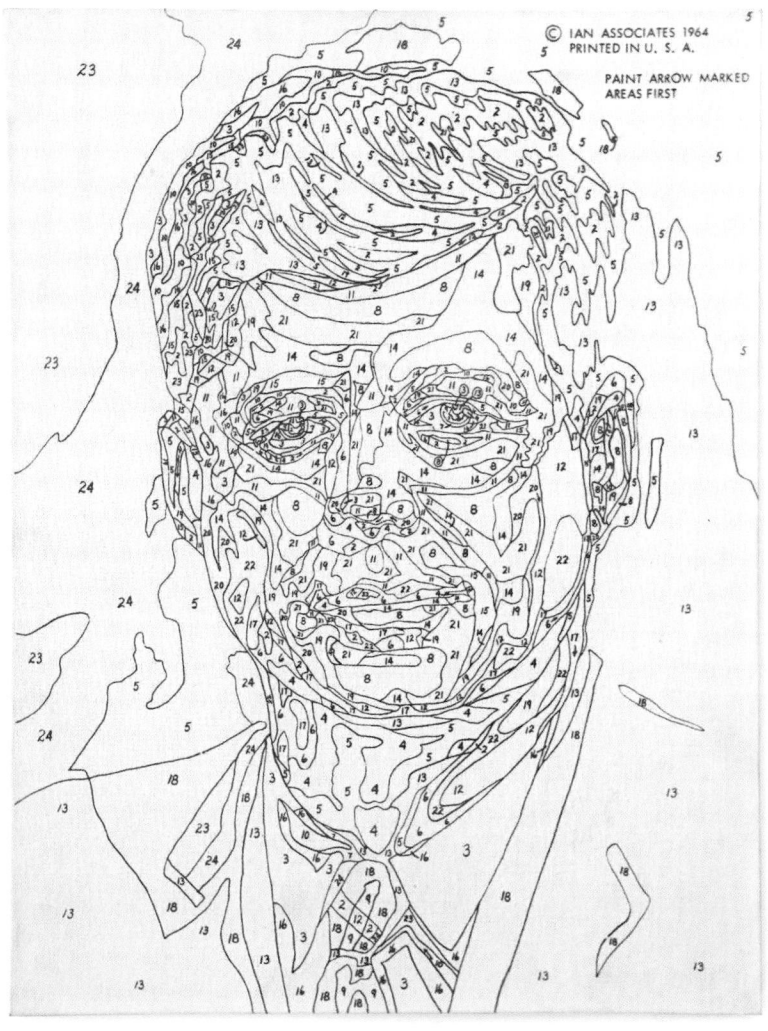

JOHN F. KENNEDY PAINT-BY-NUMBER, 1964, United States,
ink printed on canvas board, 18" x 12", collection of John and Teenuh Foster

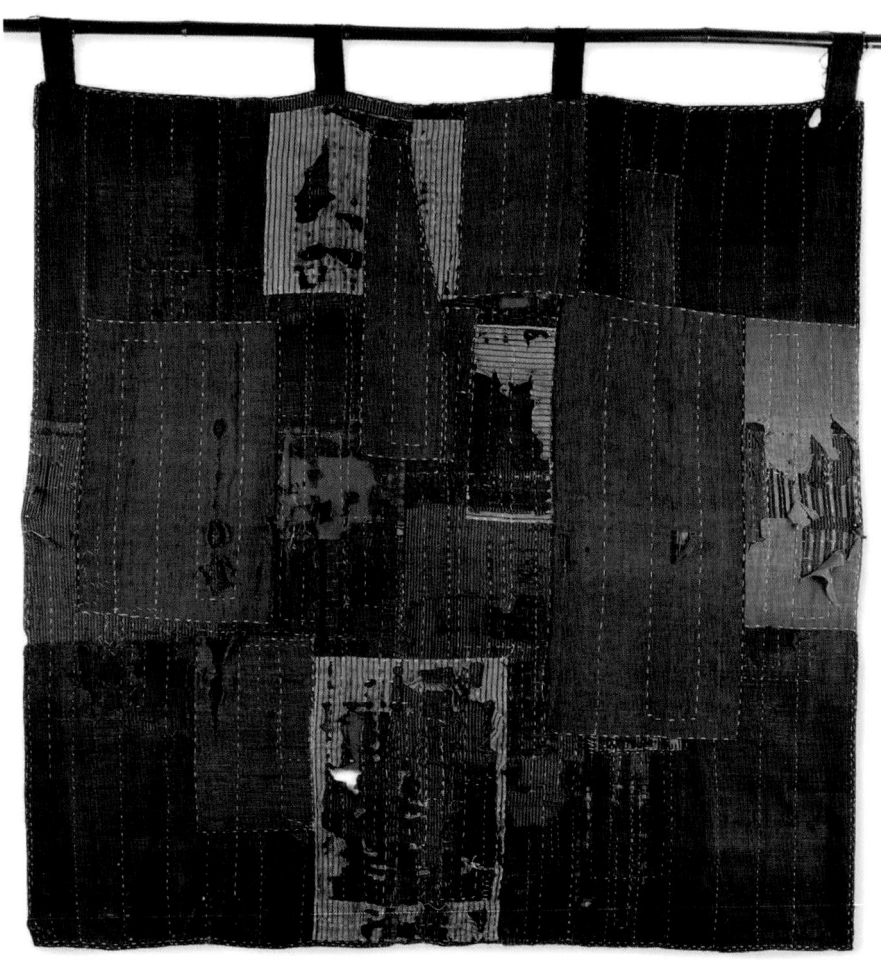

BORO (futon cover), before 1945, Japan, indigo dye, cotton,
56" x 56", collection of Shari Cavin and Randall Morris

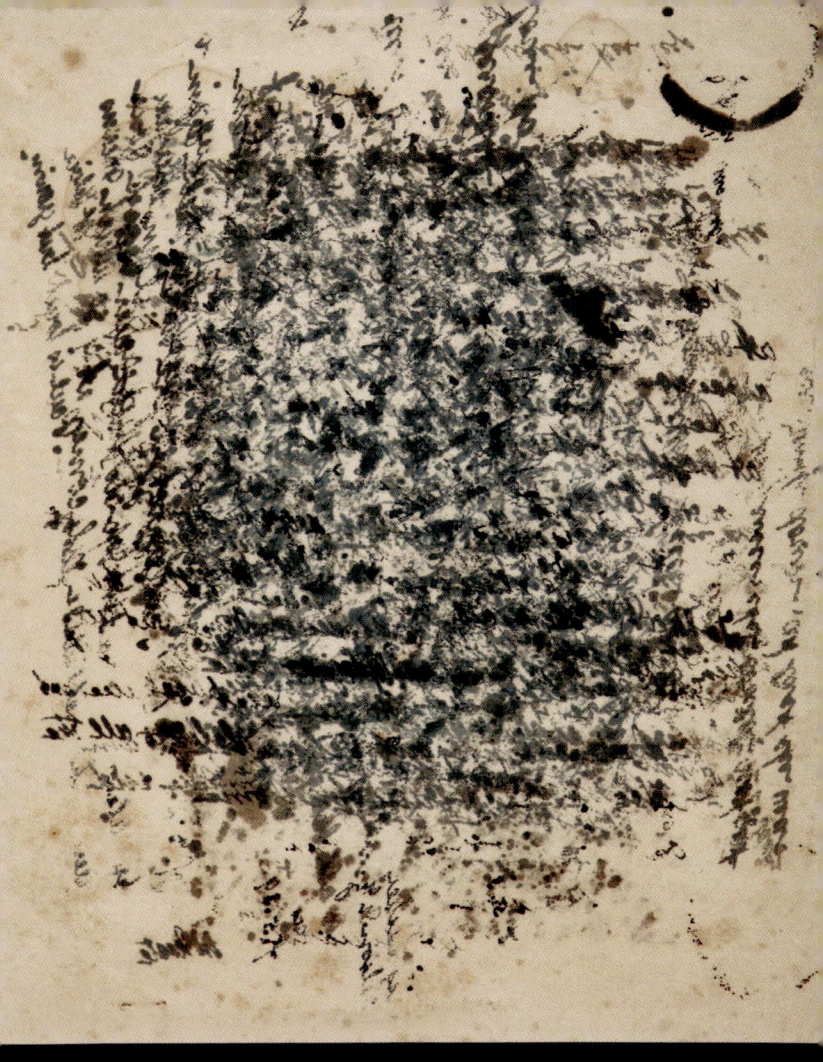

LETTER BLOTTER SHEET, 19th century, United States, ink on heavy

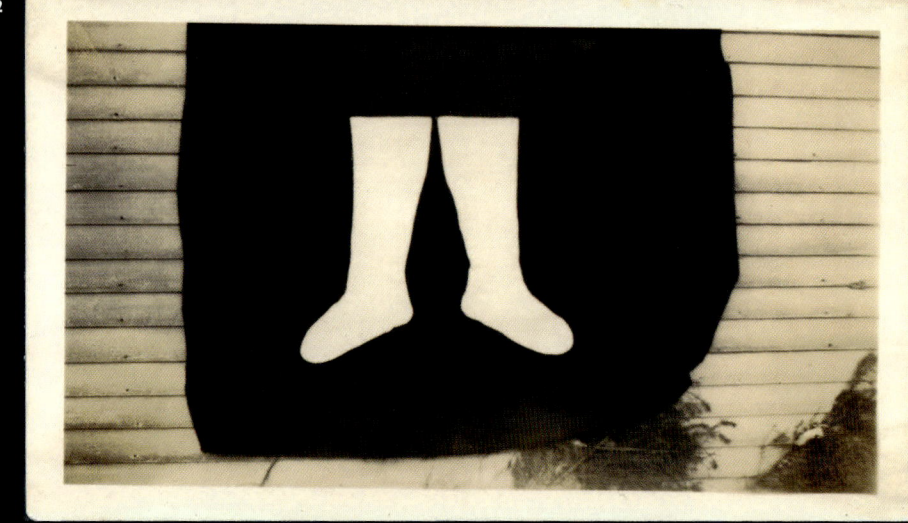

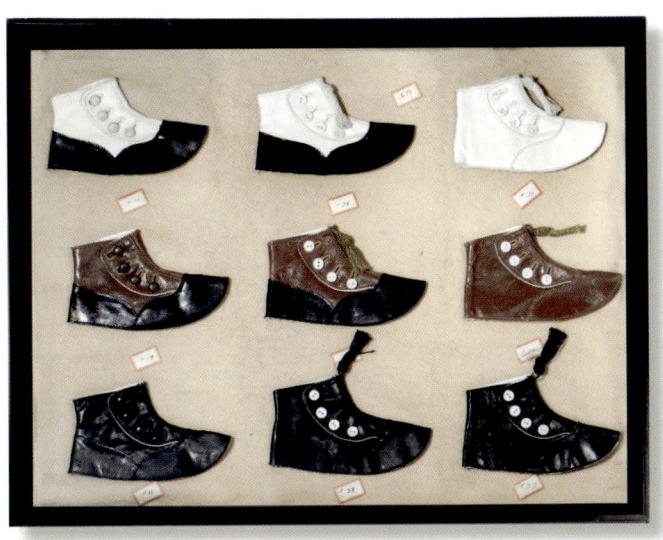

STORE DISPLAY OF CHILDREN'S SPATS, c. 1920, England, leather, buttons, 12" x 17", collection of Steve Erenberg

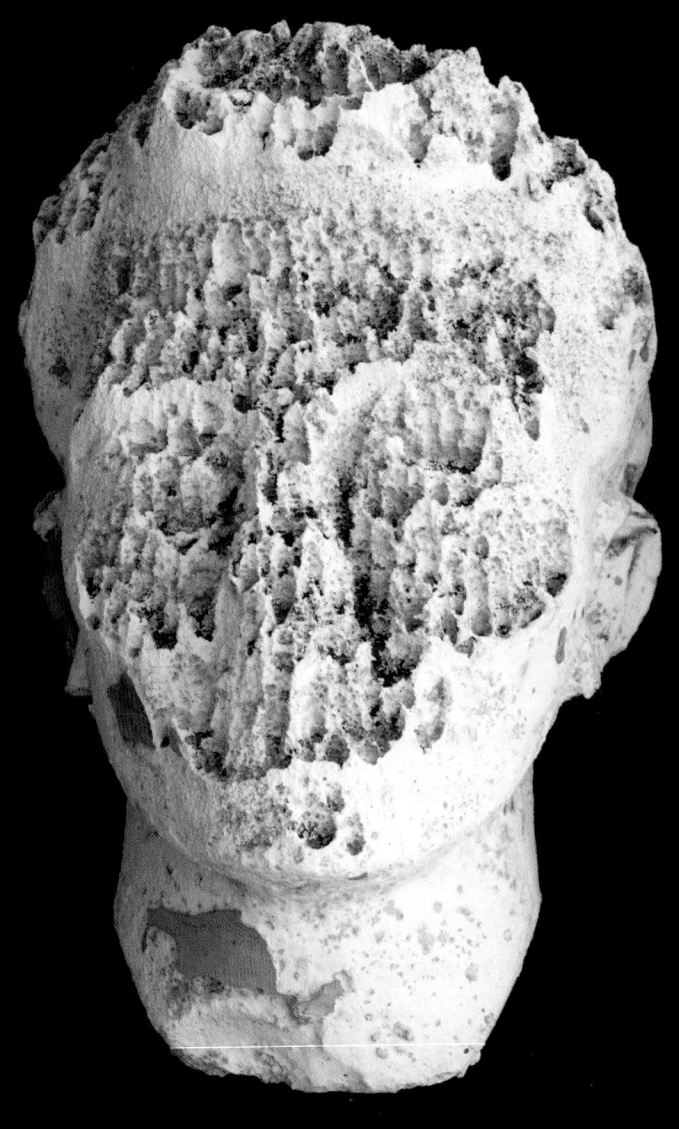

ANONYMOUS PLASTER HEAD, c. 1950, United States,
rain-damaged plaster, 14" x 8" x 12", collection of John and Teenuh Foster

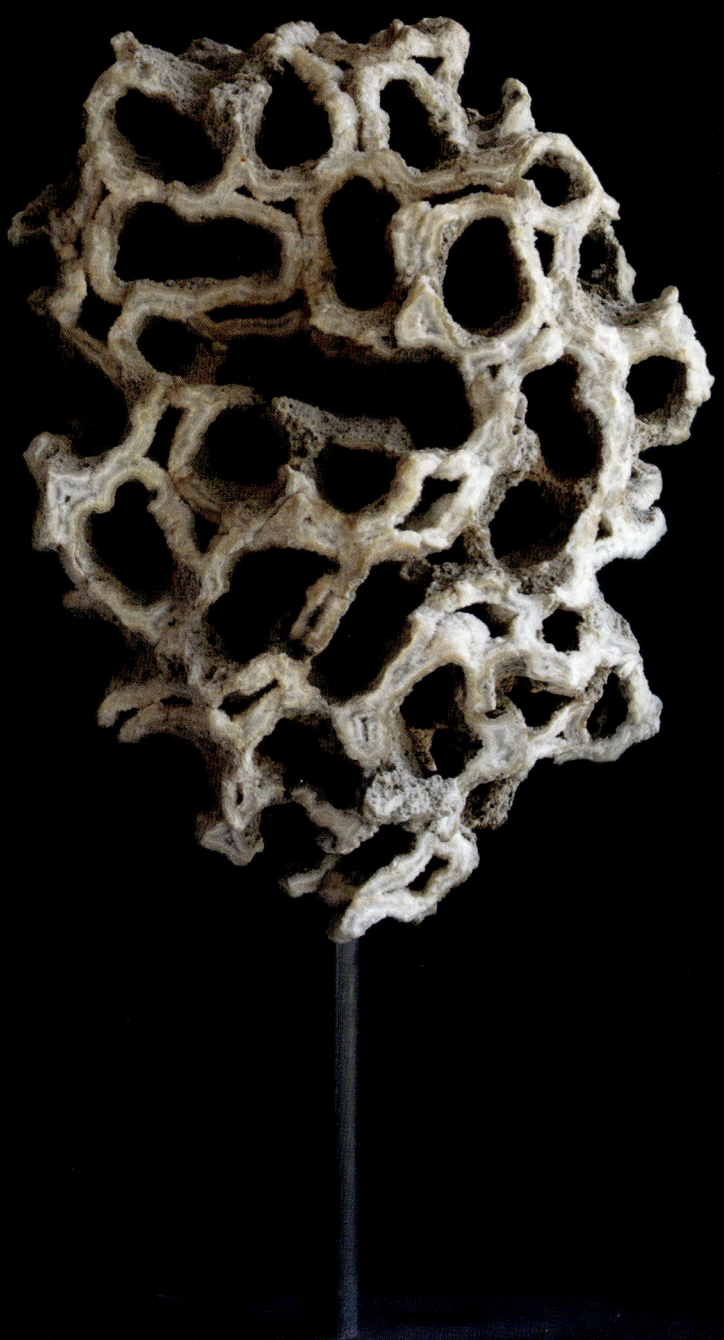

MISSOURI RIVER ROCK, United States, found natural stone,
12" x 11" x 8", collection of John and Teenuh Foster

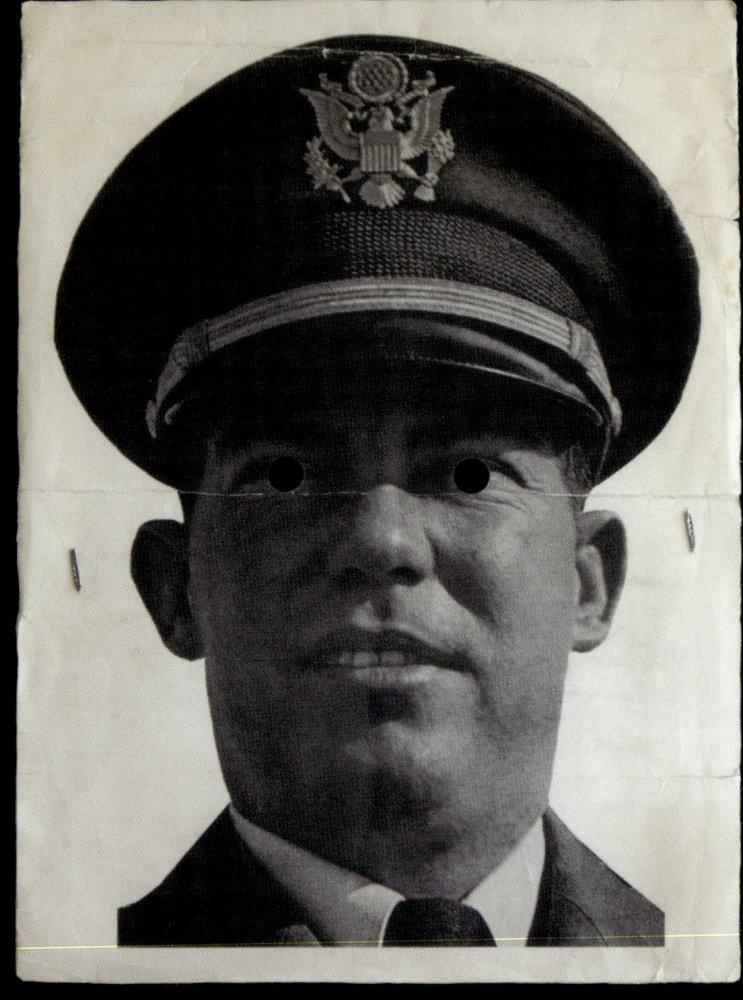

WAR PROTEST MASK OF LT. WILLIAM L. CALLEY, JR.,
1968, United States, offset print on paper, die-cut eyeholes, elastic, 12 ½" x 9 ½
collection of John and Teenuh Foster

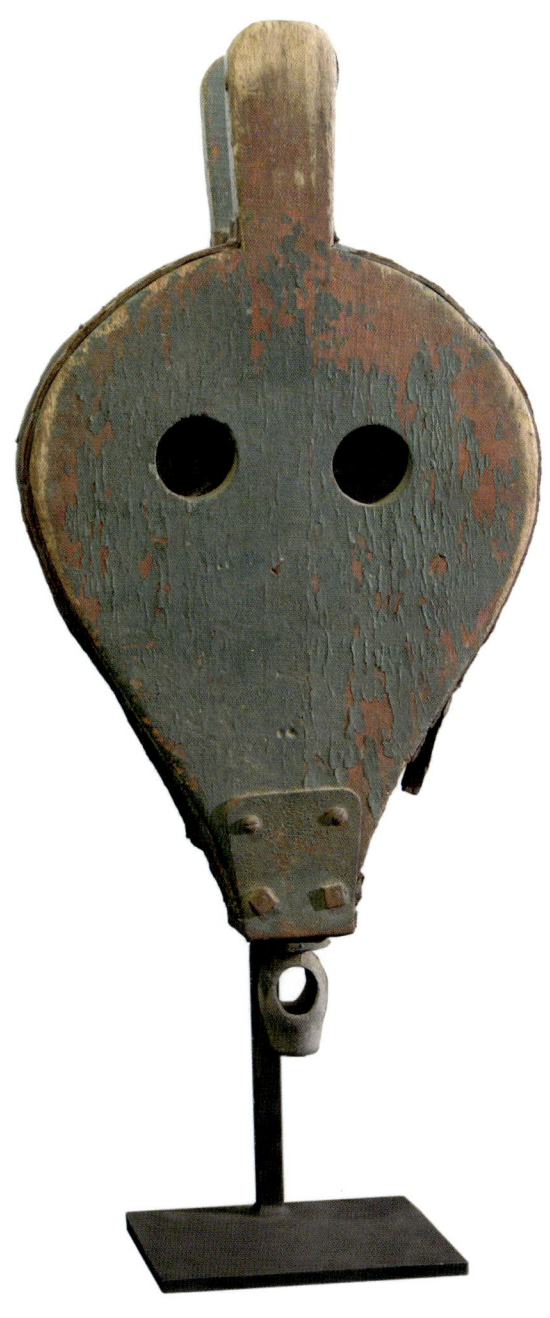

FIREPLACE BELLOWS, 19th century, United States, painted wood, leather, metal,
23" x 9", collection of American Primitive Gallery, New York

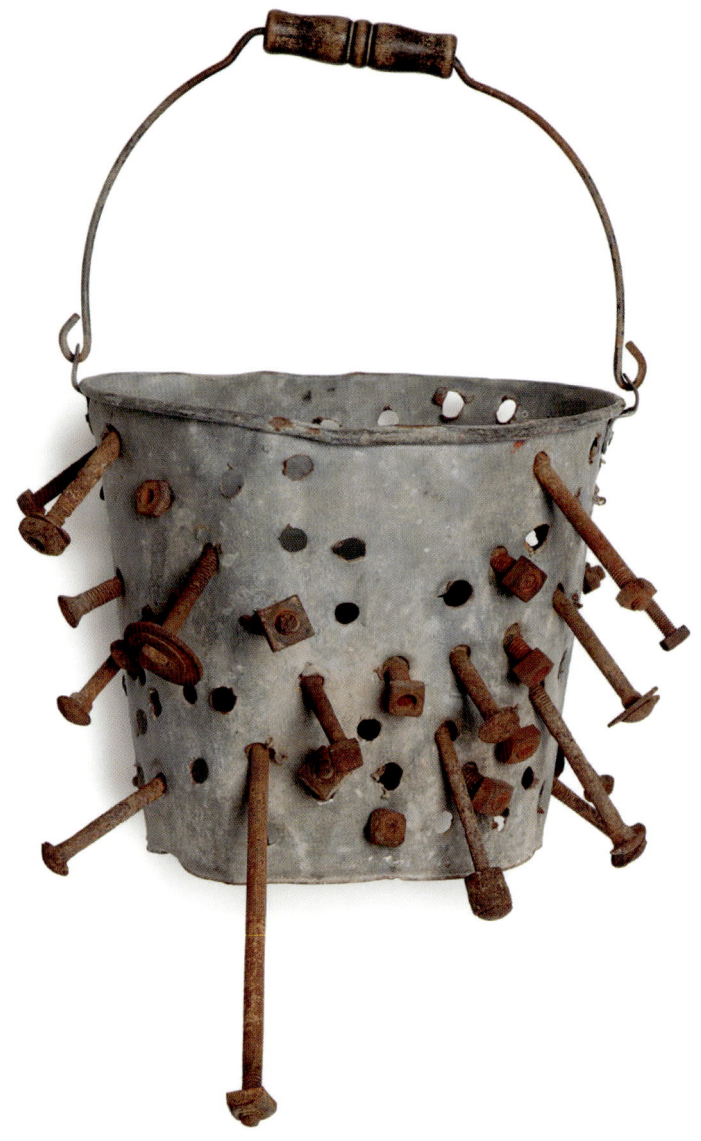

IMPROVISED CHIMNEY CLEANING DEVICE, c. 1940s, United States, galvanized bucket, wood, iron bolts, 13" x 10" diameter, collection of Rick Ege

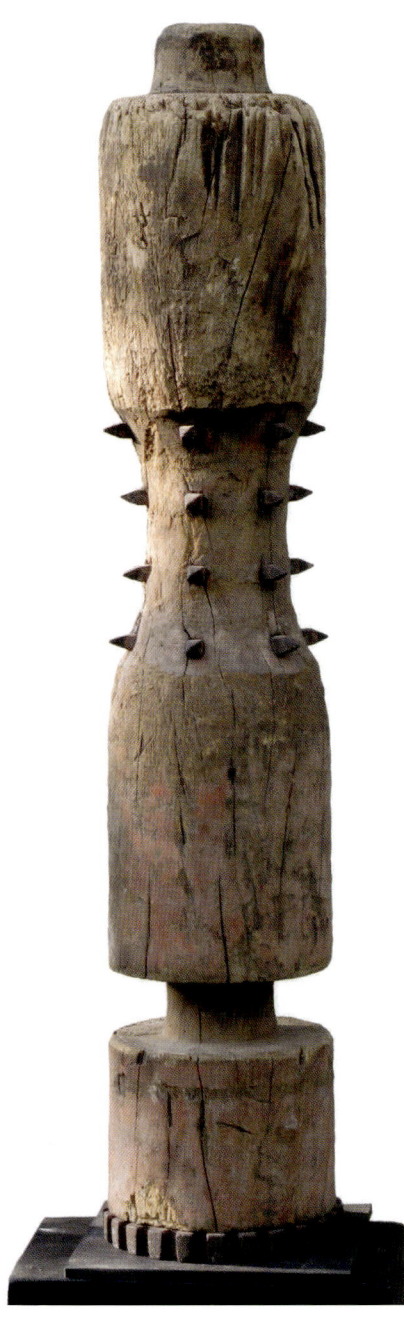

GRINDING MILL POST, 19th century, United States, painted wood with
embedded iron spurs, 39" x 7" x 7", collection of American Primitive Gallery, New York

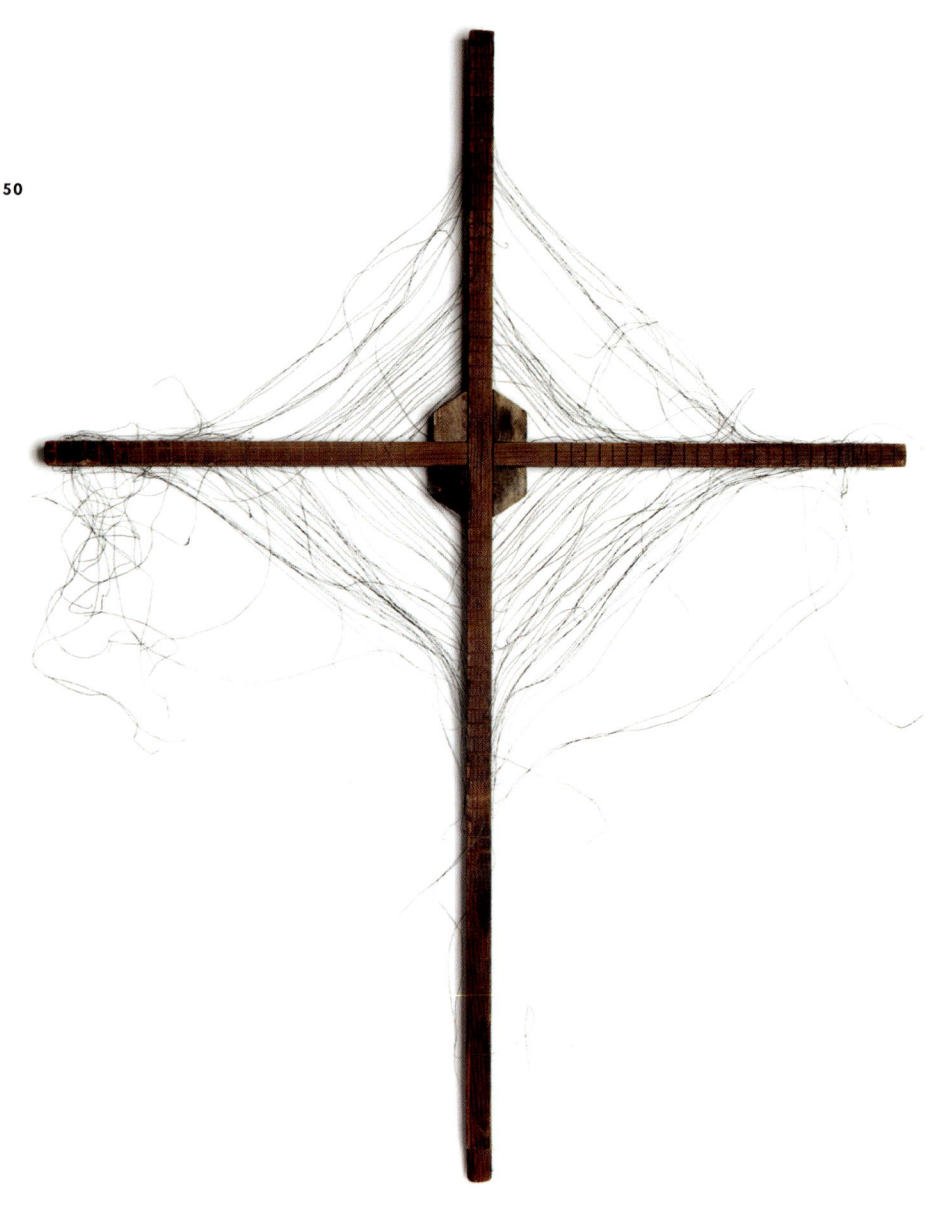

HANDMADE RADIO ANTENNA, c. 1925, United States,
incised wood, wire, 44" x 36", collection of Rick Ege

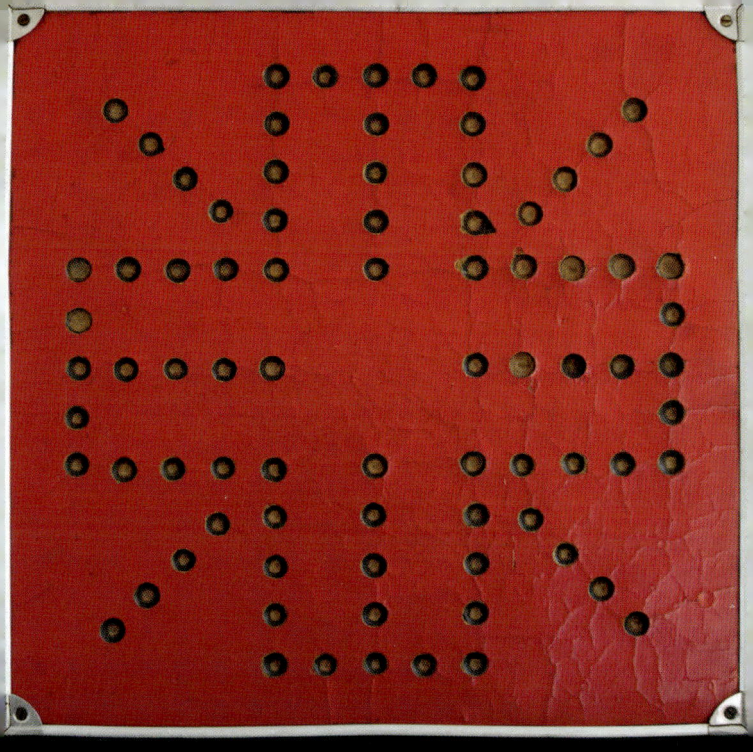

HOMEMADE GAME BOARD, c. 1950, United States, counter top linoleum,

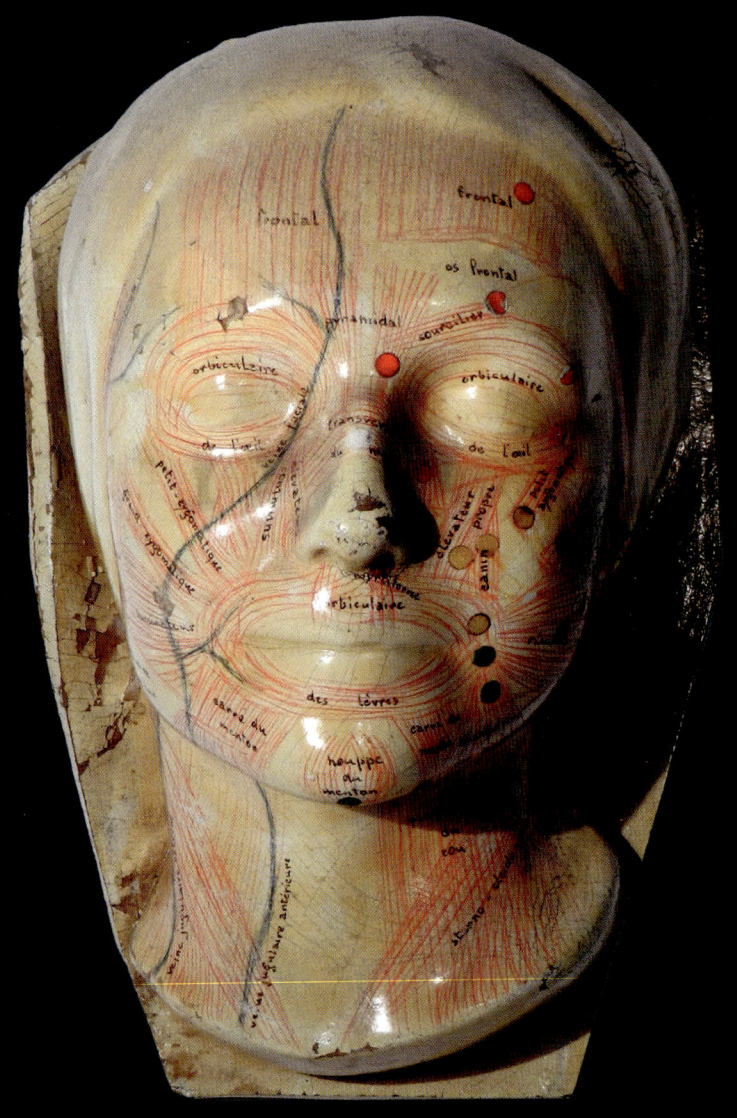

ANONYMOUS DEATH MASK *L'INCONNUE DE LA SEINE*, c. 1920s, France, hard rubber, 12" x 8" x 6", collection of Steve Erenberg

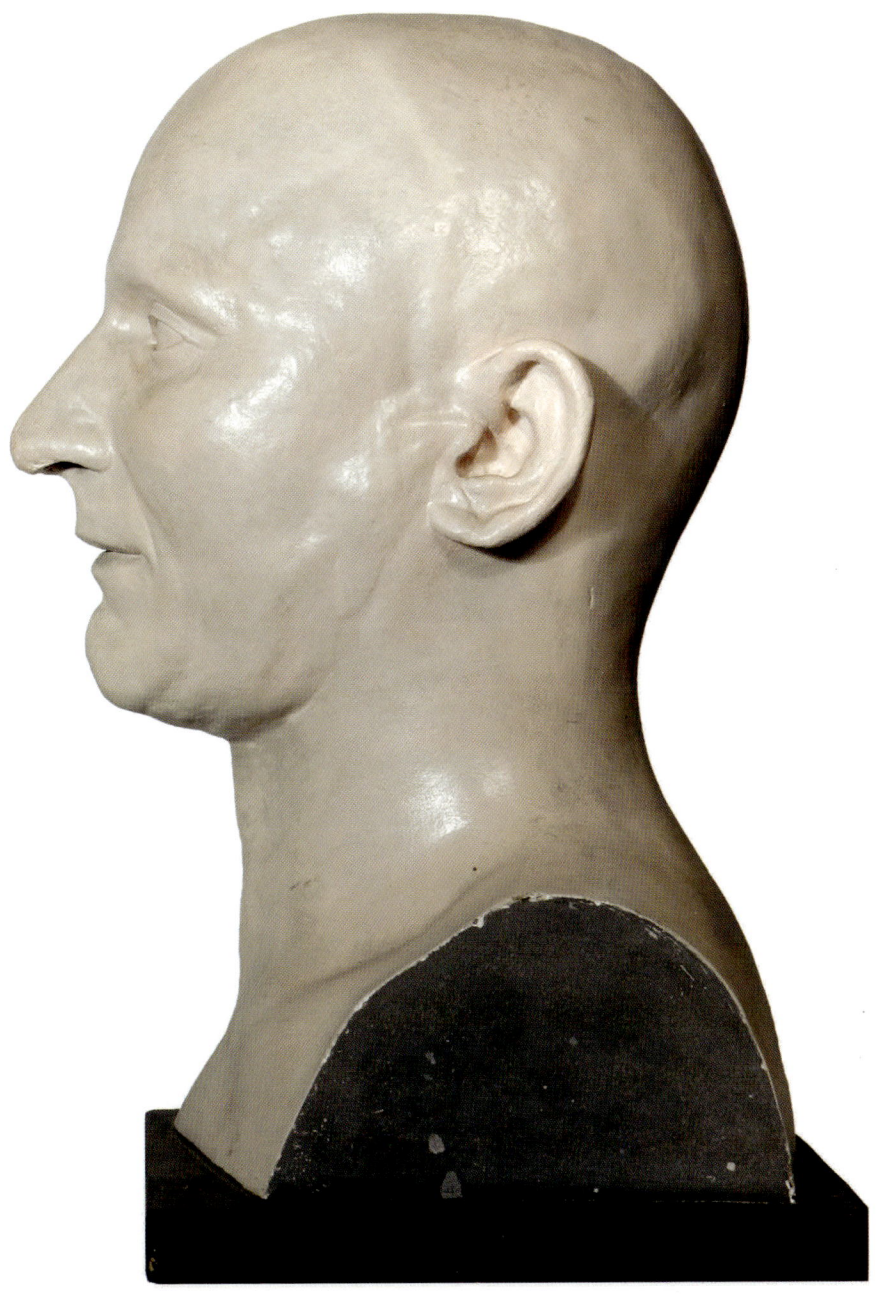

ANATOMICAL SECTION OF HEAD AND NECK (exterior), c. 1880, Germany, plaster, 14" x 9" x 8", collection of Steve Erenberg; cast from life.

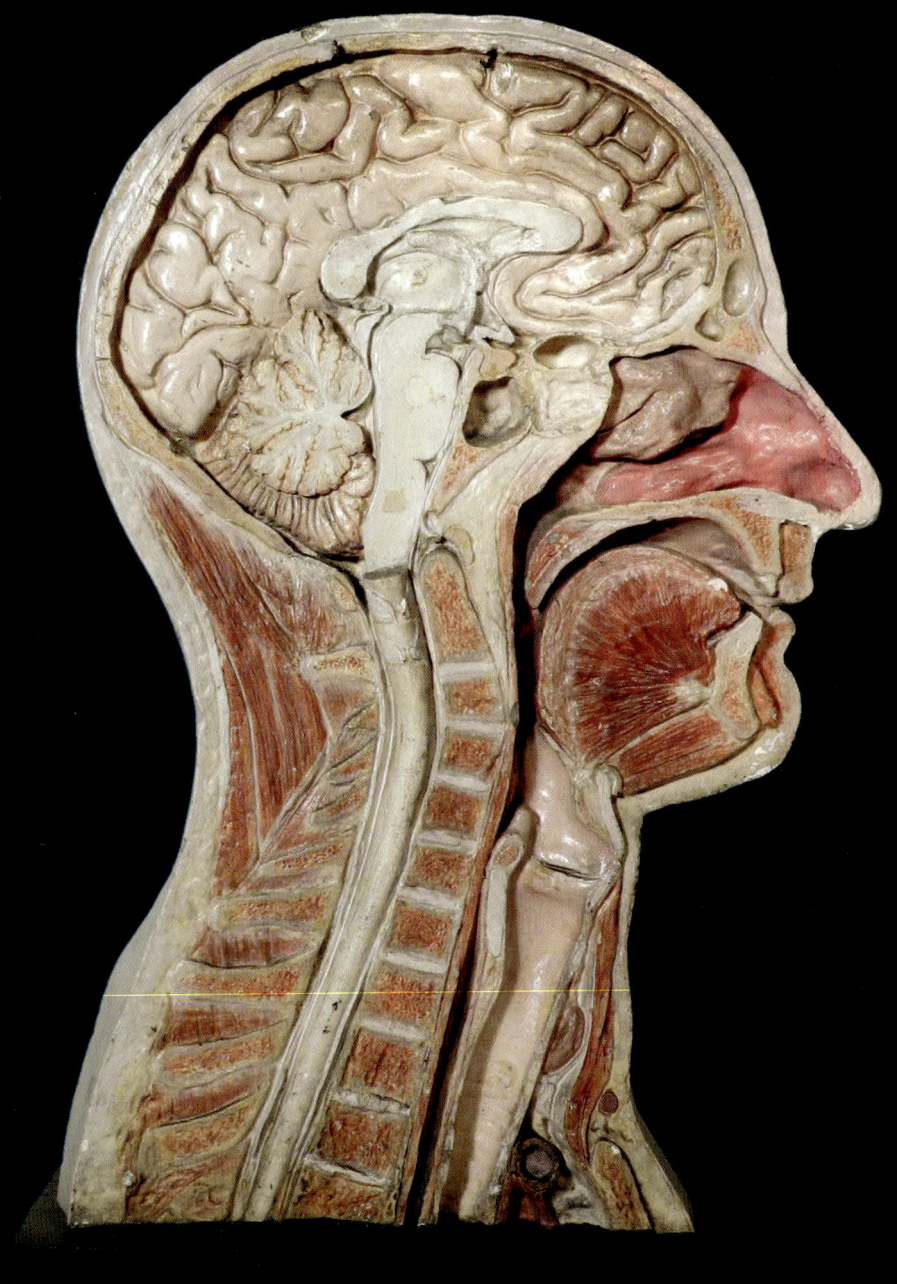

ANATOMICAL SECTION OF HEAD AND NECK (interior view), c. 1880, Germany,
plaster, 14" x 9" x 8", collection of Steve Erenberg

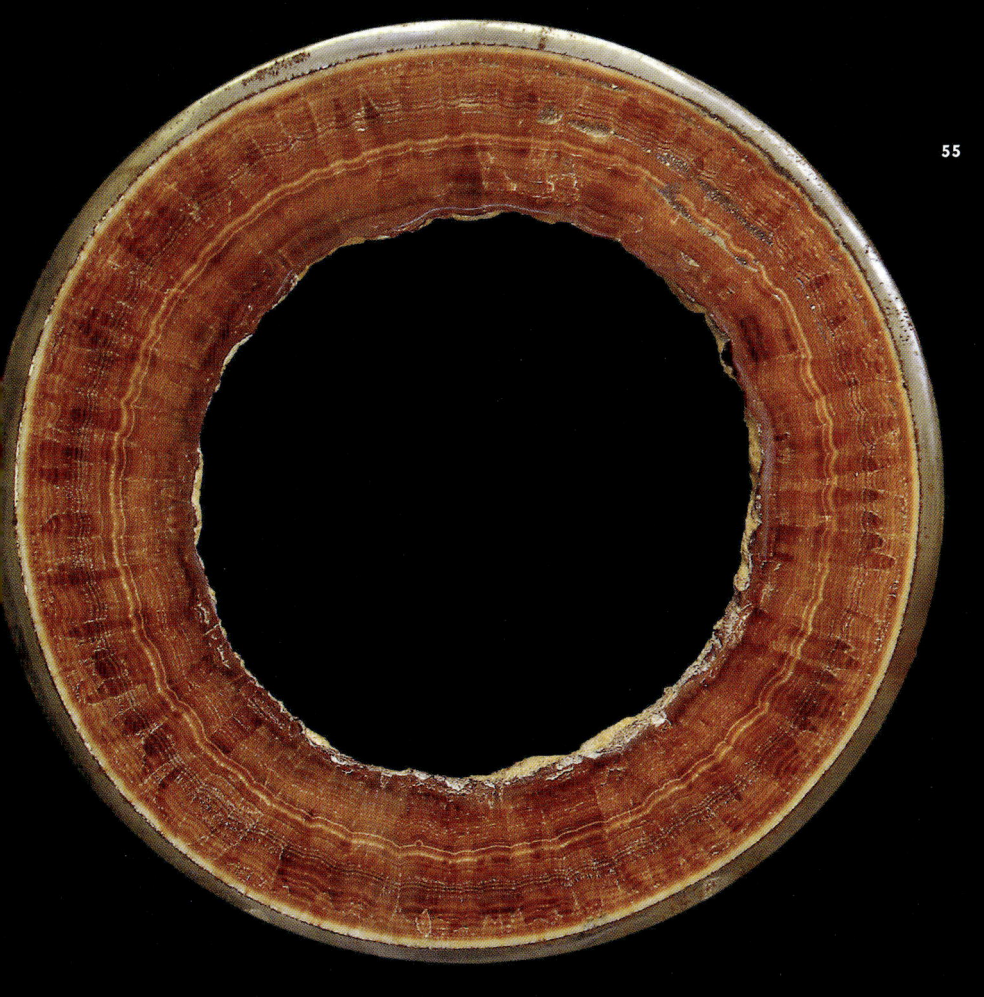

AGATIZED WATER PIPE, c. 1990, Czech Republic, steel, mineralized silica deposits, 12 ¼" diameter, collection of Jim Goodnight

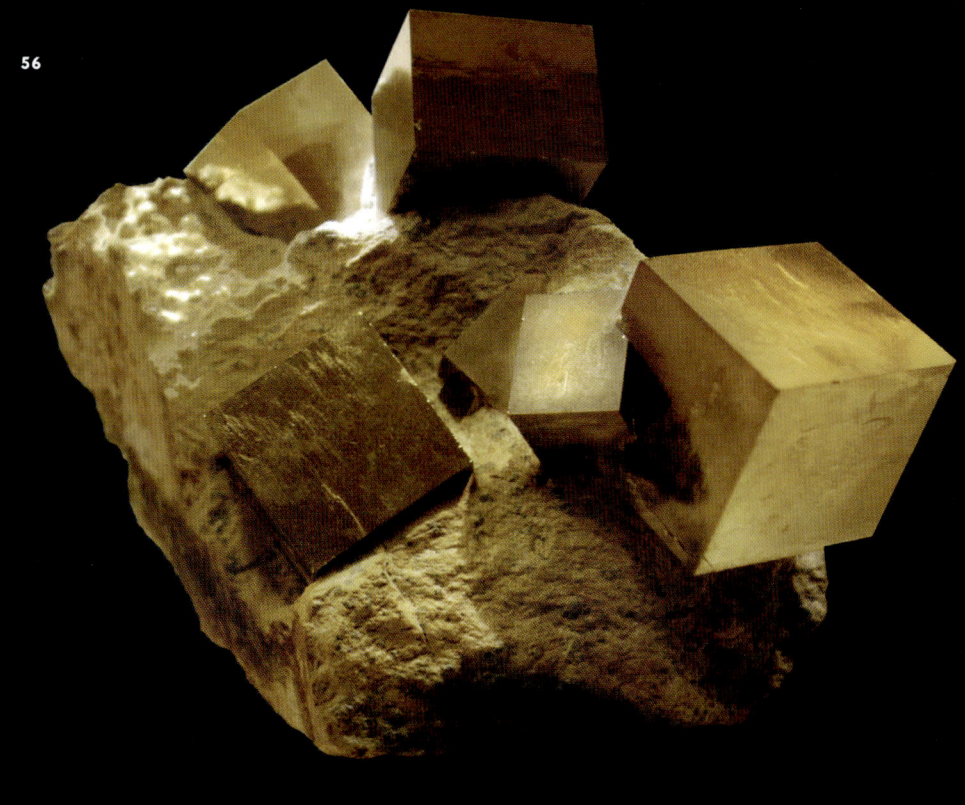

NAVAJUN FOOL'S GOLD, Spain, natural object,
iron pyrite crystals, 5 ½" x 7 ¼" x 7", collection of Jim Goodnight

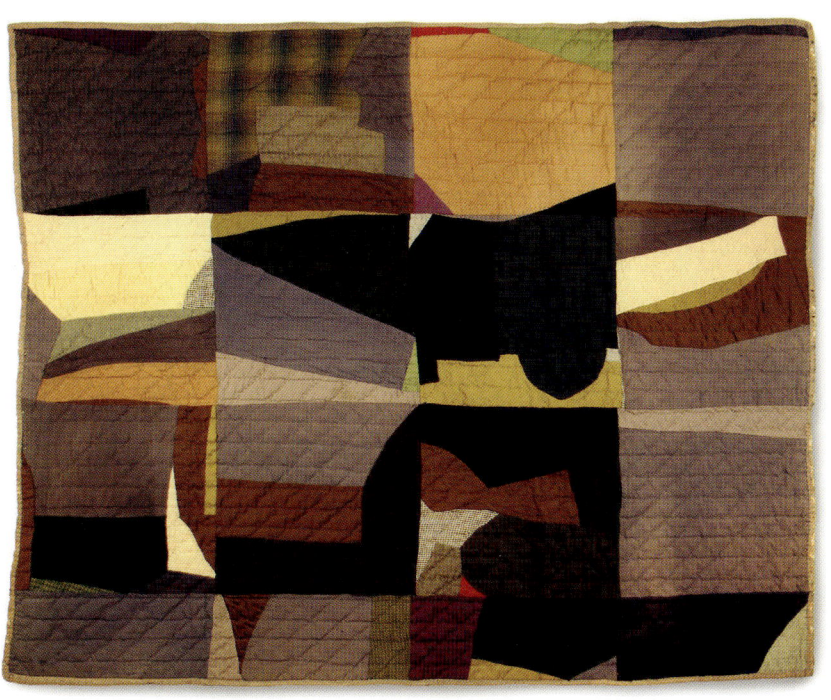

CRAZY QUILT, c. 1920–50, United States, cotton batting, pieced cotton and wool top, 62" x 72", Gregg Museum collection, gift of A. Everette James Jr. and Dr. Nancy J. Farmer

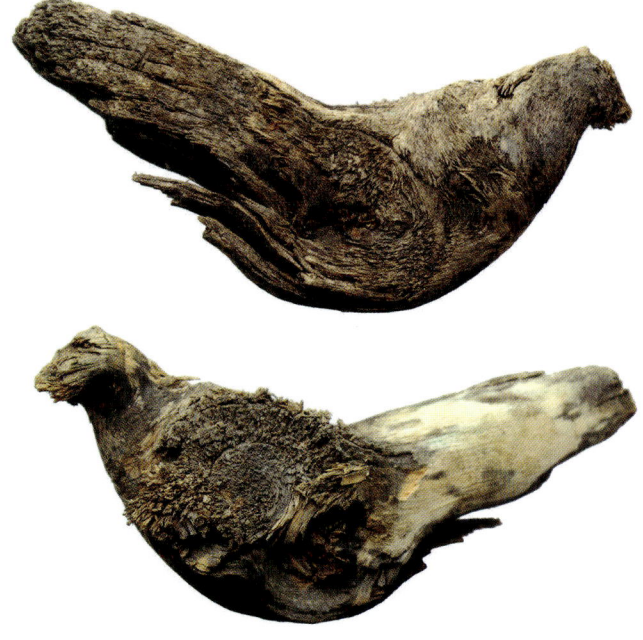

PINE-KNOT BIRD, United States, natural object, found wood knot,
3" x 2" x 7", collection of William Brack

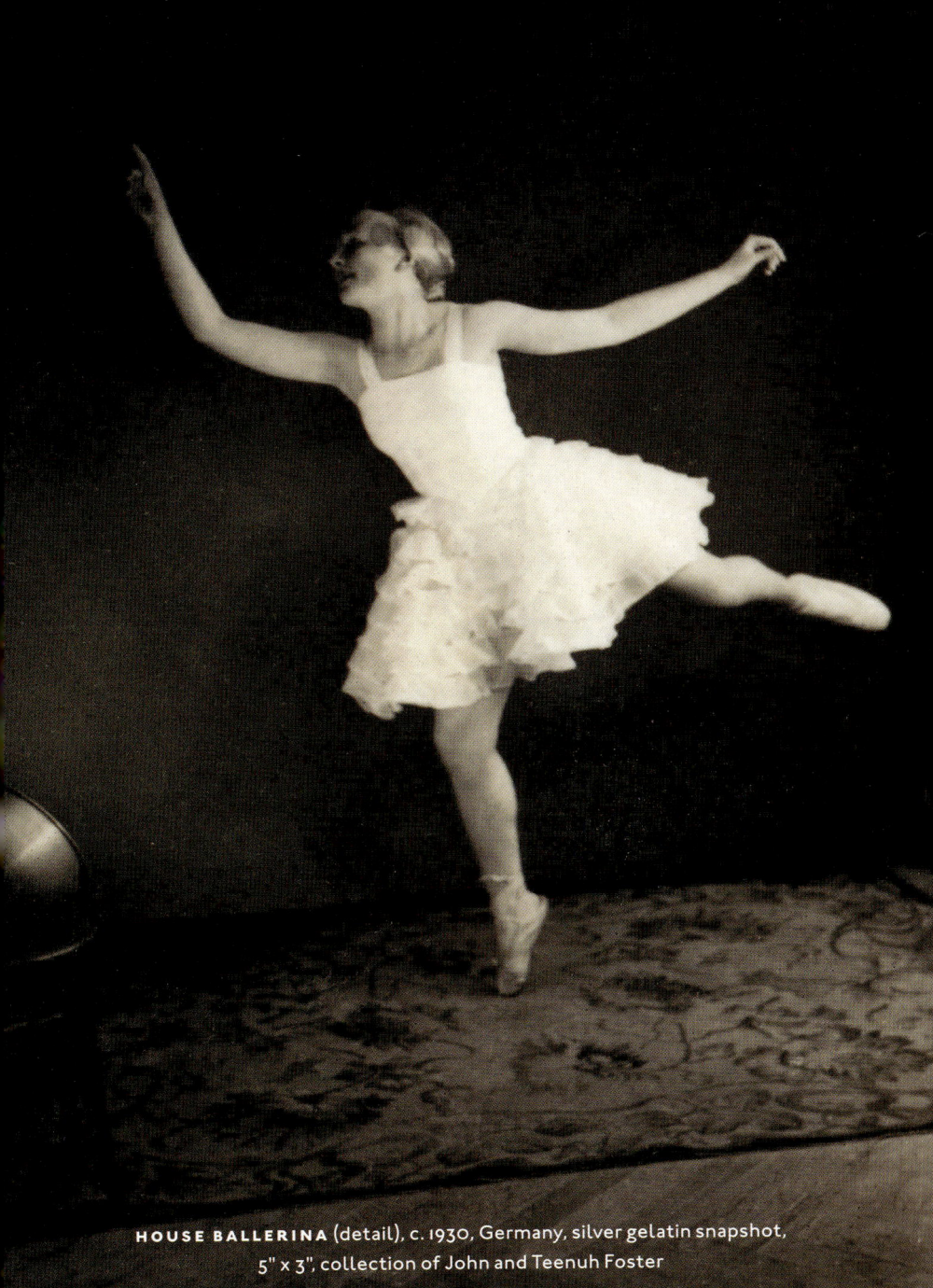

HOUSE BALLERINA (detail), c. 1930, Germany, silver gelatin snapshot,
5" x 3", collection of John and Teenuh Foster

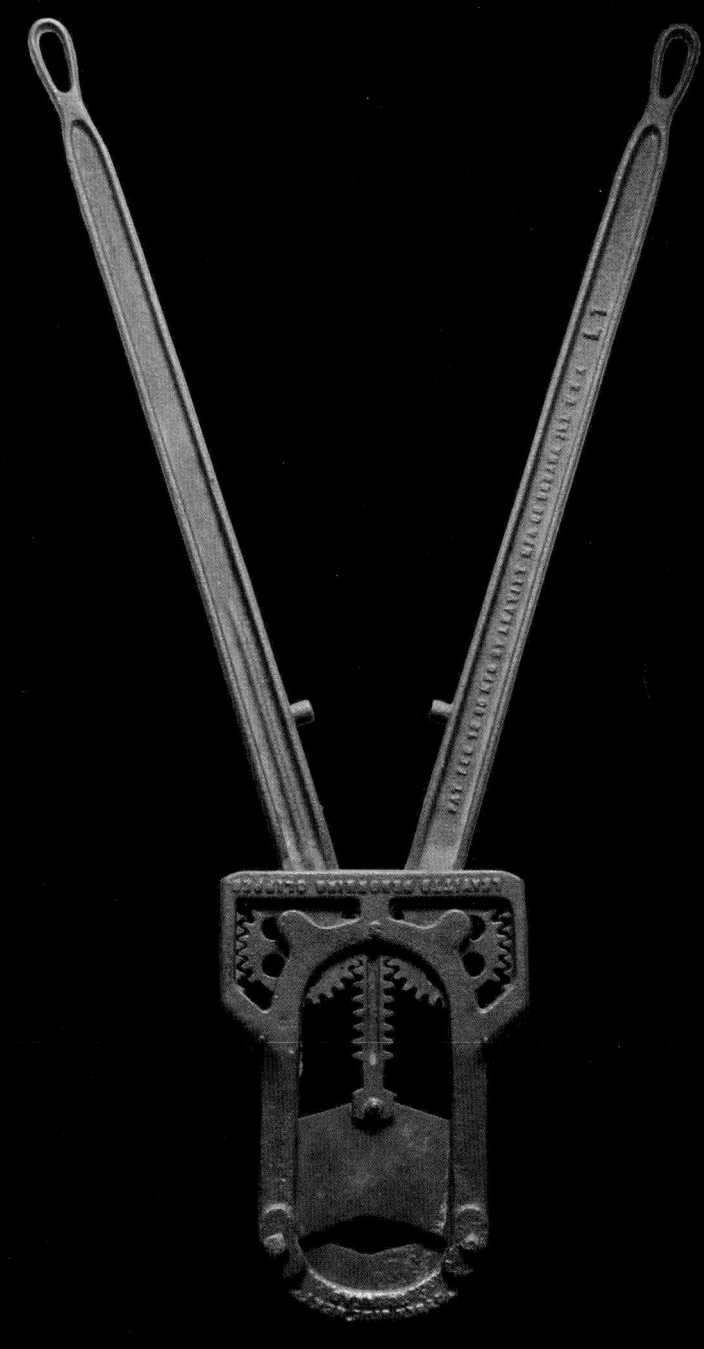

ANIMAL HORN CLIPPER, 19th century, United States, iron,
37" x 8" x 1", collection of American Primitive Gallery, New York

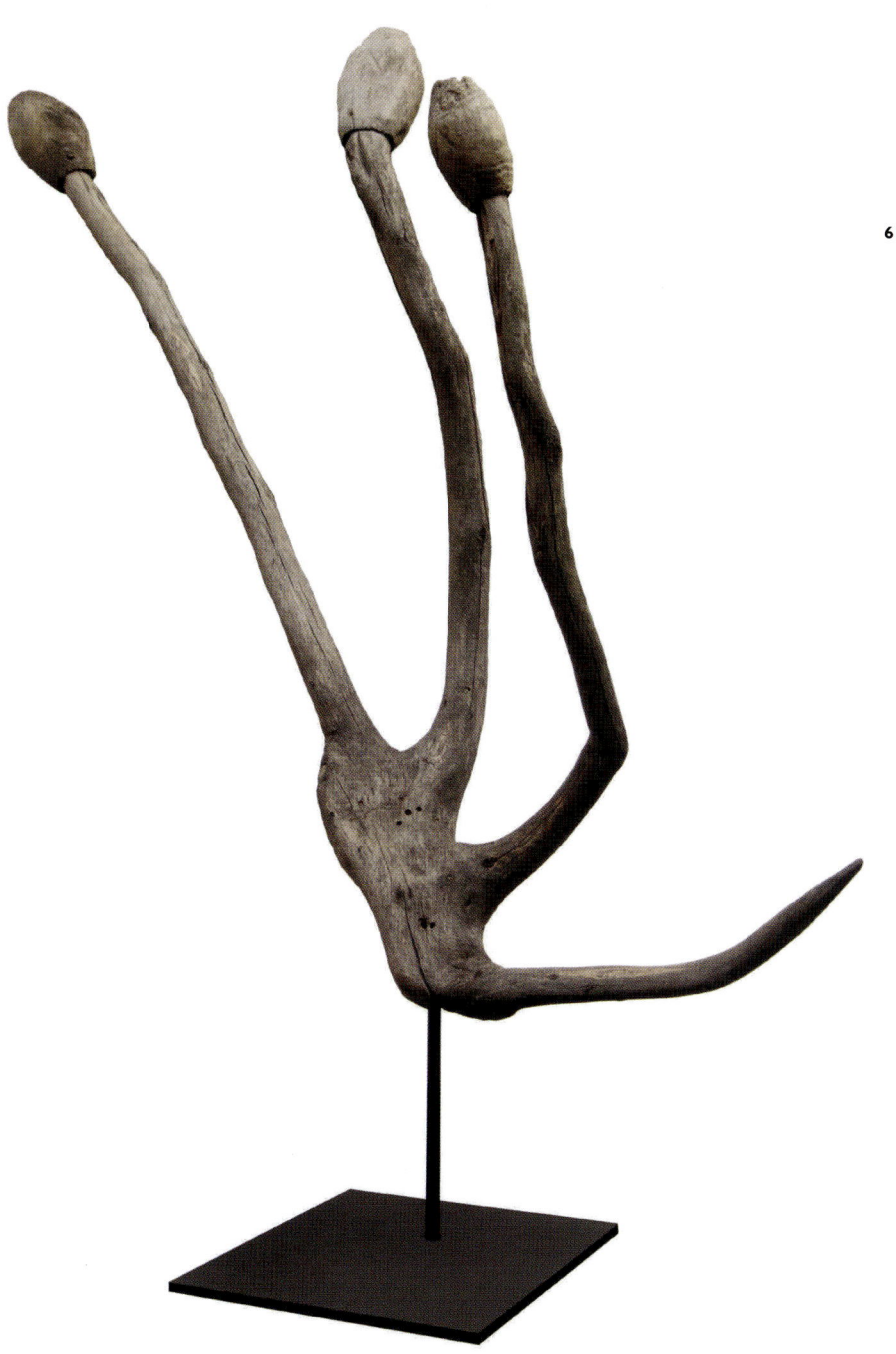

HOMEMADE TACK HOLDER, 19th century, United States,
wood, putty, 24" x 24" x 8", American Primitive Gallery, New York, NY

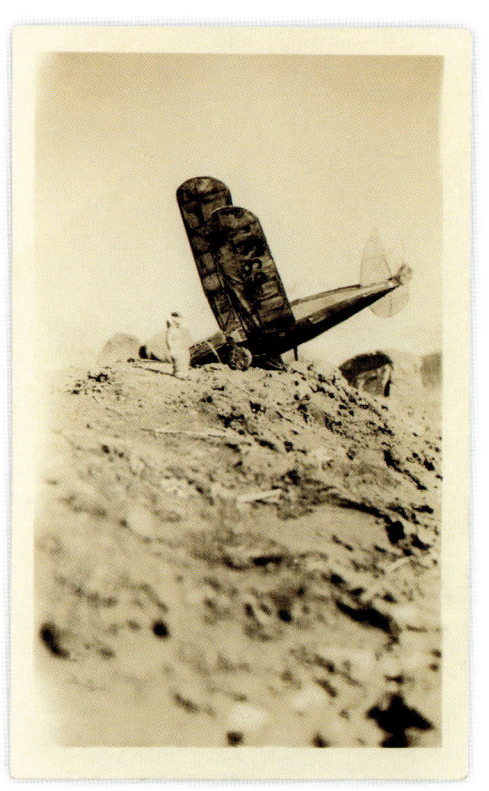

TOY PLANE CRASH SITE, c. 1940, United States,
silver gelatin snapshot, 5" x 3", collection of John and Teenuh Foster

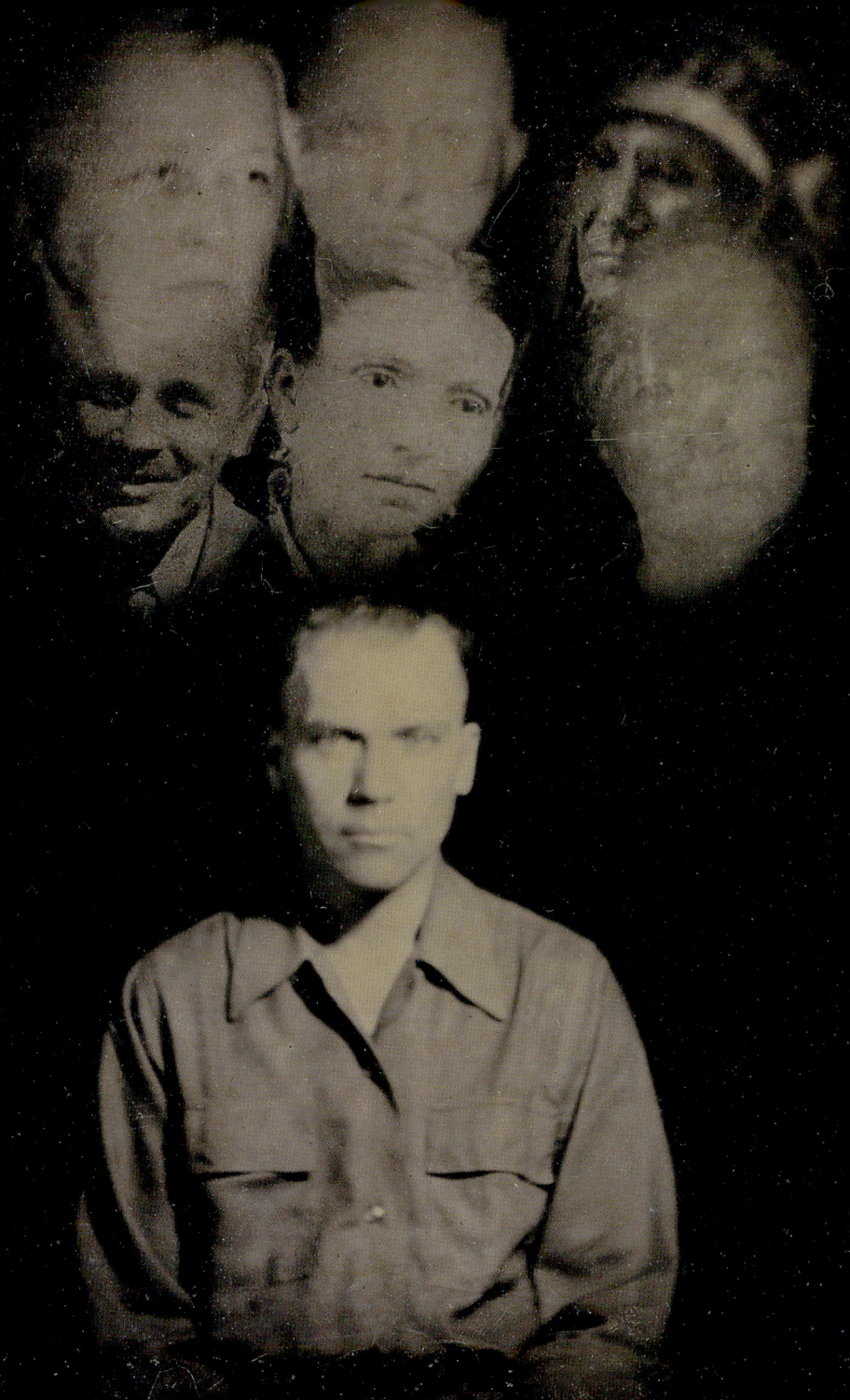

YOUR ANCESTORS ARE HERE, c. 1925, anonymous "spirit" image, United States, silver gelatin photograph, 6" x 4", collection of John and Teenuh Foster

MISSION STATEMENT

North Carolina State University's Gregg Museum of Art & Design collects, interprets and exhibits exemplary hand and machine-made objects to foster learning and understanding of the cultures of North Carolina and the world.

MUSEUM STAFF

Roger Manley, *Director*

Zoe Starling, *Curator of Education*

Mary Hauser, *Registrar*

Chris Gannon, *Assistant Registrar*

Matt Gay, *Art Preparator*

Hilary Kinlaw, *Museum
Operations Manager*

Clara Ray and Catherine Nuzum,
Security and Reception

Janine LeBlanc, *Textiles Consultant*

FRIENDS OF THE GREGG BOARD

Jim Clark, *President*

Jon W. Bartley, *Secretary/Treasurer*

Pam Bostic

Larry Campbell

Marie Cordella

Cynthia Deis

Lisa Dickson, *Student Member*

Daniel Ellison

Bernard Hyman, *President-Elect*

Lucy Inman

Lou Johanson

Beth Khalifa

Laura Lineberger, *Student Member*

Marsha Orgeron

Steve Popson

Kathleen Rieder

Miriam Sauls

Mary Ann Scherr

William Singer

John N. Wall

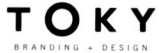

BRANDING + DESIGN

At TOKY, we believe our world can be more thoughtful, more humane, and more beautiful. Through our strategic design and communications work, we help the organizations that create this world be more successful. TOKY.COM

   NC STATE UNIVERSITY | 125 YEARS

GREGG MUSEUM OF ART & DESIGN

North Carolina State University, Campus Box 7306, Raleigh, NC 27695-7306
For more information about the Gregg Museum of Art & Design, please visit
www.ncsu.edu/gregg | 919.515.3503